Linux Observability with BPF
Advanced Programming for Performance Analysis and Networking

David Calavera and Lorenzo Fontana

Beijing · Boston · Farnham · Sebastopol · Tokyo

Linux Observability with BPF

by David Calavera and Lorenzo Fontana

Published by O'Reilly Media, Inc., 1005 Gravenstein Highway North, Sebastopol, CA 95472.

O'Reilly books may be purchased for educational, business, or sales promotional use. Online editions are also available for most titles (*http://oreilly.com*). For more information, contact our corporate/institutional sales department: 800-998-9938 or *corporate@oreilly.com*.

Acquisitions Editor: John Devins	**Indexer:** Ellen Troutman
Development Editor: Melissa Potter	**Interior Designer:** David Futato
Production Editor: Katherine Tozer	**Cover Designers:** Karen Montgomery, Suzy Wiviott
Copyeditor: Kim Wimpsett	**Illustrator:** Rebecca Demarest
Proofreader: Octal Publishing, LLC	

October 2019:   First Edition

Revision History for the First Edition

2019-10-15:   First Release

See *http://oreilly.com/catalog/errata.csp?isbn=9781492050209* for release details.

978-1-492-05020-9

[LSI]

Table of Contents

Foreword

As a programmer (and a self-confessed dweeb), I like to stay up to date on the latest additions to various kernels and research in computing. When I first played around with Berkeley Packet Filter (BPF) and Express Data Path (XDP) in Linux, I was in love. These are such nice tools, and I am glad this book is putting BPF and XDP on the center stage so that more people can begin using them in their projects.

Let me go into detail about my background and why I fell in love with these kernel interfaces. I was working as a Docker core maintainer, along with David. Docker, if you are not familiar, shells out to `iptables` for a lot of the filtering and routing logic for containers. The first patch I ever made to Docker was to fix a problem in which a version of `iptables` on CentOS didn't have the same command-line flags, so writing to `iptables` was failing. There were a lot of weird issues like this, and anyone who has ever shelled out to a tool in their software can likely commiserate. Not only that, but having thousands of rules on a host is not what `iptables` was built for and results in performance side effects.

Then I heard about BPF and XDP. This was like music to my ears. No longer would my scars from `iptables` bleed with another bug! The kernel community is even working on replacing `iptables` with BPF (*https://oreil.ly/cuqTy*)! Hallelujah! Cilium (*https://cilium.io*), a tool for container networking, is using BPF and XDP for the internals of its project as well.

But that's not all! BPF can do so much more than just fulfilling the `iptables` use case. With BPF, you can trace any syscall or kernel function as well as any user-space program. bpftrace (*https://github.com/iovisor/bpftrace*) gives users DTrace-like abilities in Linux from their command line. You can trace all the files that are being opened and the process calling the open ones, count the syscalls by the program calling them, trace the OOM killer, and more...the world is your oyster! BPF and XDP are also used in Cloudflare (*https://oreil.ly/OZdmj*) and Facebook's load balancer (*https:// oreil.ly/wrM5-*) to prevent distributed denial-of-service attacks. I won't spoil why

XDP is so great at dropping packets because you will learn about that in the XDP and networking chapters of this book!

I have had the privilege of knowing Lorenzo through the Kubernetes community. His tool, `kubectl-trace` (*https://oreil.ly/Ot7kq*), allows users to easily run their custom tracing programs within their Kubernetes clusters.

Personally, my favorite use case for BPF has been writing custom tracers to prove to other folks that the performance of their software is not up to par or makes a really expensive number of calls to syscalls. Never underestimate the power of proving someone wrong with hard data. Don't fret, this book will walk you through writing your first tracing program so that you can do the same. The beauty of BPF lies in the fact that before now other tools used lossy queues to send sample sets to user-space for aggregation, whereas BPF is great for production because it allows for constructing histograms and filtering directly at the source of events.

I have spent half of my career working on tools for developers. The best tools allow autonomy in their interfaces for developers like you to use them for things even the authors never imagined. To quote Richard Feynman, "I learned very early the difference between knowing the name of something and knowing something." Until now you might have only known the name BPF and that it might be useful to you.

What I love about this book is that it gives you the knowledge you need to be able to create all new tools using BPF. After reading and following the exercises, you will be empowered to use BPF like a super power. You can keep it in your toolkit to use on demand when it's most needed and most useful. You won't just learn BPF; you will understand it. This book is a path to open your mind to the possibilities of what you can build with BPF.

This developing ecosystem is very exciting! I hope it will grow even larger as more people begin wielding BPF's power. I am excited to learn about what the readers of this book end up building, whether it's a script to track down a crazy software bug or a custom firewall or even infrared decoding (*https://lwn.net/Articles/759188*). Be sure to let us all know what you build!

— *Jessie Frazelle*

Preface

In 2015, David was working as a core developer for Docker, the company that made containers popular. His day-to-day work was divided between helping the community and growing the project. Part of his job was reviewing the firehose of pull requests that members of the community sent us; he also had to ensure that Docker worked for all kinds of scenarios, including high-performance workloads that were running and provisioning thousands of containers at any point of time.

To diagnose performance issues at Docker, we used *flame graphs*, which are advanced visualizations to help you navigate that data easily. The Go programming language makes it really easy to measure and extract application performance data using an embedded HTTP endpoint and generate graphs based on that data. David wrote an article about Go's profiler capabilities and how you can use its data to generate flame graphs. A big pitfall about the way that Docker collects performance data is that the profiler is disabled by default, so if you're trying to debug a performance issue, the first action to take is to restart Docker. The main issue with this strategy is that by restarting the service, you'll probably lose the relevant data that you're trying to collect, and then you need to wait until the event you're trying to trace happens again. In David's article about Docker flame graphs, he mentioned this as a necessary step to measure Docker's performance, but that it didn't need to be this way. This realization made him start researching different technologies to collect and analyze any application's performance, which led him to discover BPF.

In the meantime, but far from David, Lorenzo was looking for a reason to better study the Linux kernel internals, and he discovered that it was easy to get to know many kernel subsystems by approaching them while learning about BPF. A couple of years later, he was able to apply BPF at his job at InfluxData to understand ways to make the data ingestion faster in InfluxCloud. Now Lorenzo is involved in the BPF community and IOVisor, and he works at Sysdig on Falco, a tool that uses BPF to do runtime security for containers and Linux.

Over the past few years, we've used BPF in multiple scenarios, from gathering utilization data from Kubernetes clusters to managing network traffic policies. We've learned its ins and outs by using it and by reading many blog posts from technology leaders like Brendan Gregg and Alexei Starovoitov and companies like Cilium and Facebook. Their articles and publications helped us tremendously in the past, and they have also been a huge reference for the development of this book.

After reading many of those resources, we realized that every time we needed to learn something about BPF, we needed to jump between many blog posts, man pages, and other places on the internet. This book is our attempt to put the knowledge scattered across the web in a central location for the next generation of BPF enthusiasts to learn about this fantastic technology.

We've divided our work between nine different chapters to show you what you can accomplish by using BPF. You can read some chapters in isolation as reference guides, but if you're new to BPF, we recommend you to read them in order. That will give you an overview of the core concepts in BPF and guide you through the possibilities ahead of you.

Whether you're already an expert in observability and performance analysis or you're researching new possibilities to answer questions about your production systems that you couldn't solve before, we hope you find new knowledge in this book.

Conventions Used in This Book

The following typographical conventions are used in this book:

Italic
Indicates new terms, URLs, email addresses, filenames, and file extensions.

`Constant width`
Used for program listings, as well as within paragraphs to refer to program elements such as variable or function names, databases, data types, environment variables, statements, and keywords.

`Constant width bold`
Shows commands or other text that should be typed literally by the user.

`Constant width italic`
Shows text that should be replaced with user-supplied values or by values determined by context.

This element signifies a tip or suggestion.

 This element signifies a general note.

 This element indicates a warning or caution.

Using Code Examples

Supplemental material (code examples, exercises, etc.) is available for download at *https://oreil.ly/lbpf-repo*.

This book is here to help you get your job done. In general, if example code is offered with this book, you may use it in your programs and documentation. You do not need to contact us for permission unless you're reproducing a significant portion of the code. For example, writing a program that uses several chunks of code from this book does not require permission. Selling or distributing examples from O'Reilly books does require permission. Answering a question by citing this book and quoting example code does not require permission. Incorporating a significant amount of example code from this book into your product's documentation does require permission.

We appreciate, but do not require, attribution. An attribution usually includes the title, author, publisher, and ISBN. For example: "*Linux Observability with BPF* by David Calavera and Lorenzo Fontana (O'Reilly). Copyright 2020 David Calavera and Lorenzo Fontana, 978-1-492-05020-9."

If you feel your use of code examples falls outside fair use or the permission given here, feel free to contact us at *permissions@oreilly.com*.

O'Reilly Online Learning

 For over 40 years, *O'Reilly Media* has provided technology and business training, knowledge, and insight to help companies succeed.

Our unique network of experts and innovators share their knowledge and expertise through books, articles, conferences, and our online learning platform. O'Reilly's online learning platform gives you on-demand access to live training courses, in-depth learning paths, interactive coding environments, and a vast collection of text and video from O'Reilly and 200+ other publishers. For more information, please visit *http://oreilly.com*.

How to Contact Us

Please address comments and questions concerning this book to the publisher:

O'Reilly Media, Inc.
1005 Gravenstein Highway North
Sebastopol, CA 95472
800-998-9938 (in the United States or Canada)
707-829-0515 (international or local)
707-829-0104 (fax)

We have a web page for this book, where we list errata, examples, and any additional information. You can access this page at *https://oreil.ly/linux-bpf*.

Email *bookquestions@oreilly.com* to comment or ask technical questions about this book.

For more information about our books, courses, conferences, and news, see our website at *http://www.oreilly.com*.

Find us on Facebook: *http://facebook.com/oreilly*

Follow us on Twitter: *http://twitter.com/oreillymedia*

Watch us on YouTube: *http://www.youtube.com/oreillymedia*

Acknowledgments

Writing a book is more difficult than we thought, but it was probably one of the most rewarding activities we have done in our lives. Many days and nights went into this book, and it would have not been possible without the help of our partners, families, friends, and dogs. We'd like to thank Debora Pace, Lorenzo's girlfriend, and his son, Riccardo, for all the patience they had waiting for him during long writing sessions. Thanks also to Lorenzo's friend Leonardo Di Donato for all the advice provided and in particular for writing about XDP and testing.

We're eternally grateful to Robin Means, David's wife, for proofreading early drafts of several chapters and the initial overview that started this book and for helping him write many articles over the years and laughing at his made-up English words that sounded cuter than they really were.

We both want to say a big thank you to all those who made eBPF and BPF possible. To David Miller and Alexei Starovoitov for their continuous contributions to improve the Linux kernel and ultimately eBPF and the community around it. To Brendan Gregg for his willing to share, his enthusiasm, and his work on tooling that make eBPF more accessible to everyone. To the IOVisor group for their vibes, emails, and all the work they put into bpftrace, gobpf, kubectl-trace, and BCC. To Daniel Borkmann for all his inspirational work, in particular on libbpf and the tools infrastructure. To Jessie Frazelle for writing the foreword and being inspirational to both of us and to thousands of developers out there. To Jérôme Petazzoni for being the best technical reviewer we could want; his questions made us rethink many parts of this book and our approach to the code examples in it.

And thank you to all the thousands of Linux kernel contributors, in particular the ones active in the BPF mailing list, for their questions/answers, their patches, and their initiatives. Finally, to all those who have been part of publishing this book at O'Reilly, including our editors, John Devins and Melissa Potter, and all the people behind the scenes who made the cover, reviewed the pages, and made this book be more professional than anything else we have done in our careers.

## CHAPTER 1

Introduction

Over the past few decades computing systems have only grown in complexity. Reasoning about how software behaves has created multiple business categories, all of them trying solve the challenges of gaining insight into complex systems. One approach to get this visibility is to analyze the logs of data generated by all applications running in a computing system. Logs are a great source of information. They can give you precise data about how an application is behaving. However, they constrain you because you get only the information that the engineers who built the application exposed in those logs. Gathering any additional information in log format from any system can be as challenging as decompiling the program and looking at the execution flow. Another popular approach is to use metrics to reason why a program behaves the way it does. Metrics differ from logs in the data format; whereas logs give you explicit data, metrics aggregate data to measure how a program behaves at a specific point in time.

Observability is an emergent practice that approaches this problem from an different angle. People define observability as the capacity that we have to ask arbitrary questions and receive complex answers from any given system. A key difference between observability, logs, and metrics aggregation is the data that you collect. Given that by practicing observability you need to answer any arbitrary question at any point in time, the only way to reason about data is by collecting all of the data that your system can generate and aggregating it only when it's necessary to answer your questions.

Nassim Nicholas Taleb, the author of best-seller books like *Antifragile: Things That Gain From Disorder* (Penguin Random House), popularized the term *Black Swan* for unexpected events, with major consequences, that could have been expected if they had been observed before they happened. In his book *The Black Swan* (Penguin Random House), he rationalizes how having relevant data could help in risk mitigation for these rare events. Black Swan events are more common than we think in software engineering, and they are inevitable. Because we can assume that we cannot prevent these kinds of events, our only option is to have as much information as possible about them to address them without affecting business systems in a critical way. Observability helps us build robust systems and mitigate future Black Swan events because it's based on the premise that you're collecting any data that can answer any future question. The study of Black Swan events and practicing observability converges in one central point, which is in the data that you gather from your systems.

Linux containers are an abstraction on top of a set of features on the Linux kernel to isolate and manage computer processes. The kernel, traditionally in charge of resource management, also provides task isolation and security. In Linux, the main features that containers are based on are namespaces and cgroups. Namespaces are the components that isolate tasks from one another. In a sense, when you're inside a namespace, you experience the operating system like there were no other tasks running on the computer. Cgroups are the components that provide resource management. From an operational point of view, they give you fine-grained control over any resource usage, such as CPU, disk I/O, network, and so on. In the past decade, with the raise in popularity of Linux containers, there has been a shift in the way software engineers design large distributed systems and compute platforms. Multitenant computing has grown completely reliant on these features in the kernel.

By relying so much on the low-level capabilities of the Linux kernel, we've tapped into a new source of complexity and information that we need to consider when we design observable systems. The kernel is an evented system, which means that all work is described and executed based on events. Opening files is a kind of event, executing an arbitrary instruction by a CPU is an event, receiving a network packet is an event, and so on. Berkeley Packet Filter (BPF) is a subsystem in the kernel that can inspect those new sources of information. BPF allows you to write programs that are safely executed when the kernel triggers any event. BPF gives you strong safety guarantees to prevent you from injecting system crashes and malicious behavior in those programs. BPF is enabling a new wave of tools to help system developers observe and work with these new platforms.

In this book, we show you the power that BPF offers you to make any computing system more observable. We also show you how to write BPF programs with the help of multiple programming languages. We've put the code for your programs on GitHub, so you don't need to copy and paste it. You can find it in a Git repository companion to this book (*https://oreil.ly/lbpf-repo*).

But before we begin to focus on the technical aspects of BPF, let's look at how everything began.

BPF's History

In 1992, Steven McCanne and Van Jacobson wrote the paper "The BSD Packet Filter: A New Architecture for User-Level Packet Capture." In this paper, the authors described how they implemented a network packet filter for the Unix kernel that was 20 times faster than the state of the art in packet filtering at the time. Packet filters have a specific purpose: to provide applications that monitor the system's network with direct information from the kernel. With this information, applications could decide what to do with those packets. BPF introduced two big innovations in packet filtering:

- A new virtual machine (VM) designed to work efficiently with register-based CPUs.
- The usage of per-application buffers that could filter packets without copying all the packet information. This minimized the amount of data BPF required to make decisions.

These drastic improvements made all Unix systems adopt BPF as the technology of choice for network packet filtering, abandoning old implementations that consumed more memory and were less performant. This implementation is still present in many derivatives of that Unix kernel, including the Linux kernel.

In early 2014, Alexei Starovoitov introduced the extended BPF implementation. This new design was optimized for modern hardware, making its resulting instruction set faster than the machine code generated by the old BPF interpreter. This extended version also increased the number of registers in the BPF VM from two 32-bit registers to ten 64-bit registers. The increase in the number of registers, and in their width, opened the possibility to write more complex programs, because developers were free to exchange more information using function parameters. These changes, among other improvements, made the extended BPF version up to four times faster than the original BPF implementation.

The initial goal for this new implementation was to optimize the internal BPF instruction set that processed network filters. At this point, BPF was still restricted to kernel-space, and only a few programs in user-space could write BPF filters for the kernel to process, like Tcpdump and Seccomp, which we talk about in later chapters. Today, these programs still generate bytecode for the old BPF interpreter, but the kernel translates those instructions to the much improved internal representation.

In June 2014, the extended version of BPF was exposed to user-space. This was an inflection point for the future of BPF. As Alexei wrote in the patch that introduced these changes, "This patch set demonstrates the potential of eBPF."

BPF became a top-level kernel subsystem, and it stopped being limited to the networking stack. BPF programs began to look more like kernel modules, with a big emphasis on safety and stability. Unlike kernel modules, BPF programs don't require you to recompile your kernel, and they are guaranteed to complete without crashing.

The BPF verifier, which we talk about in the next chapter, added these required safety guarantees. It ensures that any BPF program will complete without crashing, and it ensures that programs don't try to access memory out of range. These advantages come with certain restrictions, though: programs have a maximum size allowed, and loops need to be bounded to ensure that the system's memory is never exhausted by a bad BPF program.

With the changes to make BPF accessible from user-space, the kernel developers also added a new system call (syscall), bpf. This new syscall will be the central piece of communication between user-space and the kernel. We discuss how to use this syscall to work with BPF programs and maps in Chapters 2 and 3 of this book.

BPF maps will become the main mechanism to exchange data between the kernel and user-space. Chapter 2 demonstrates how to use these specialized structures to collect information from the kernel as well as send information to BPF programs that are already running in the kernel.

The extended BPF version is the starting point for this book. In the past five years, BPF has evolved significantly since the introduction of this extended version, and we cover in detail the evolution of BPF programs, BPF maps, and kernel subsystems that have been affected by this evolution.

Architecture

BPF's architecture within the kernel is fascinating. We dive into its specific details through the entire book, but we want to give you a quick overview about how it works in this chapter.

As we mentioned earlier, BPF is a highly advanced VM, running code instructions in an isolated environment. In a sense, you can think of BPF like how you think about the Java Virtual Machine (JVM), a specialized program that runs machine code compiled from a high-level programming language. Compilers like LLVM, and GNU Compiler Collection (GCC) in the near future, provide support for BPF, allowing you to compile C code into BPF instructions. After your code is compiled, BPF uses a verifier to ensure that the program is safe to run by the kernel. It prevents you from running code that might compromise your system by crashing the kernel. If your code is safe, the BPF program will be loaded in the kernel. The Linux kernel also incorporates a just-in-time (JIT) compiler for BPF instructions. The JIT will transform the BPF bytecode into machine code directly after the program is verified, avoiding this overhead on execution time. One interesting aspect of this architecture is that you don't need to restart your system to load BPF programs; you can load them on demand, and you can also write your own init scripts that load BPF programs when your system starts.

Before the kernel runs any BPF program, it needs to know which execution point the program is attached to. There are multiple attachment points in the kernel, and the list is growing. The execution points are defined by the BPF program types; we discuss them in the next chapter. When you choose an execution point, the kernel also makes available specific function helpers that you can use to work with the data that your program receives, making execution points and BPF programs tightly coupled.

The final component in BPF's architecture is responsible for sharing data between the kernel and user-space. This component is called a BPF *map*, and we talk about maps in Chapter 3. BPF maps are bidirectional structures to share data. This means that you can write and read them from both sides, the kernel and user-space. There are several types of structures, from simple arrays and hash maps to specialized maps, that allow you to save entire BPF programs in them.

We cover every component in BPF's architecture in more detail as the book progresses. You'll also learn to take advantage of BPF's extensibility and data sharing, with specific examples covering topics ranging from stack trace analysis to network filtering and runtime isolation.

Conclusion

We wrote this book to help you become familar with the basic BPF concepts that you're going to need in your day-to-day work with this Linux subsystem. BPF is still a technology in development, and new concepts and paradigms are growing as we are writing this book. Ideally, this book will help you expand your knowledge easily by giving you a solid base of BPF's foundational components.

The next chapter dives directly into the structure of BPF programs and how the kernel runs them. It also covers the points in the kernel where you can attach those programs. This will help you become familiar with all the data that your programs can consume and how to use it.

## CHAPTER 2

Running Your First BPF Programs

The BPF VM is capable of running instructions in response to events triggered by the kernel. However, not all BPF programs have access to all events triggered by the kernel. When you load a program into the BPF VM, you need to decide which type of program you're running. This informs the kernel about where your program is going to be triggered. It also tells the BPF verifier which helpers are going to be allowed in your program. When you choose the program type, you're also choosing the interface that your program is implementing. This interface ensures that you have access to the appropriate type of data, and whether your program can access network packets directly or not.

In this chapter, we show you how to write your first BPF programs. We also guide you around the different types of BPF programs that you can create (as of the writing of this book). Over the years, the kernel developers have been adding different entry points to which you can attach BPF programs. This work is not complete yet, and they are finding new ways to take advantage of BPF every day. We're going to focus on some of the most useful types of programs in this chapter, with the intention of giving you a taste of what you can do with BPF. We go over many additional examples in future chapters on how to write BPF programs.

This chapter will also cover the role that the BPF verifier plays in running your programs. This component validates that your code is safe to execute and helps you to write programs that won't cause unexpected results, such as memory exhaustion or sudden kernel crashes. But let's begin with the basics of writing your own BPF programs from scratch.

Writing BPF Programs

The most common way to write BPF programs is by using a subset of C compiled with LLVM. LLVM is a general-purpose compiler that can emit different types of bytecode. In this case, LLVM will output BPF assembly code that we will load into the kernel later. We're not going to show you much BPF assembly in this book. After a long discussion, we decided that it's better to show you examples of how to use it in specific circustances, but you can easily find several references online or in the BPF man pages. We do show short examples of BPF assembly in future chapters, where writing assembly is more appropriate than C, like Seccomp filters to control incoming system calls in the kernel. We talk more about Seccomp in Chapter 8.

The kernel provides the syscall bpf to load programs into the BPF VM after they are compiled. This syscall is used for other operations besides loading programs, and you'll see more usage examples in later chapters. The kernel also provides several utilities that abstract the loading of BPF programs for you. In this first code example we use those helpers to show you the "Hello World" example of BPF:

```
#include <linux/bpf.h>
#define SEC(NAME) __attribute__((section(NAME), used))

SEC("tracepoint/syscalls/sys_enter_execve")
int bpf_prog(void *ctx) {
  char msg[] = "Hello, BPF World!";
  bpf_trace_printk(msg, sizeof(msg));
  return 0;
}

char _license[] SEC("license") = "GPL";
```

There are a few interesting concepts in this first program. We're using the attribute SEC to inform the BPF VM when we want to run this program. In this case, we will run this BPF program when a tracepoint in an execve system call is detected. Tracepoints are static marks in the kernel's binary code that allow developers to inject code to inspect the kernel's execution. We talk in detail about tracepoints in Chapter 4, but for now you need to know only that execve is an instruction that executes other programs. So we're going to see the message Hello, BPF World! every time the kernel detects that a program executes another program.

At the end of this example we also specify the license for this program. Because the Linux kernel is licensed under GPL, it can load only programs licensed as GPL too. If we set the license to something else, the kernel will refuse to load our program. We're using bpf_trace_printk to print a message in the kernel tracing log; you can find this log in */sys/kernel/debug/tracing/trace_pipe*.

We're going to use clang to compile this first program into a valid ELF binary file. This is the format that the kernel expects to load. We're going to save our first program in a file called bpf_program.c so we can compile it:

```
clang -O2 -target bpf -c bpf_program.c -o bpf_program.o
```

You'll find some scripts to compile these programs in the GitHub repository with the code example for the book (*https://oreil.ly/lbpf-repo*), so you don't need to memorize this clang command.

Now that we have compiled our first BPF program, we need to load it in the kernel. As we mentioned, we use a special helper that the kernel provides to abstract the boilerplate of compiling and loading the program. This helper is called load_bpf_file, and it takes a binary file and tries to load it in the kernel. You can find this helper in the GitHub repository with all the examples in the book (*https://oreil.ly/lbpf-repo*), in the *bpf_load.h* file, as shown here:

```
#include <stdio.h>
#include <uapi/linux/bpf.h>
#include "bpf_load.h"

int main(int argc, char **argv) {
  if (load_bpf_file("hello_world_kern.o") != 0) {
    printf("The kernel didn't load the BPF program\n");
    return -1;
  }

  read_trace_pipe();

  return 0;
}
```

We're going to use a script to compile this program and link it as an ELF binary. In this case, we don't need to specify a target, because this program won't be loaded in the BPF VM. We need to use an external library, and writing a script makes it easier to put it all together:

```
TOOLS=../../../tools
INCLUDE=../../../libbpf/include
HEADERS=../../../libbpf/src
clang -o loader -l elf \
  -I${INCLUDE} \
  -I${HEADERS} \
  -I${TOOLS} \
  ${TOOLS}/bpf_load.c \
  loader.c
```

If you want to run this program, you can execute this final binary by using sudo: sudo ./loader. sudo is a Linux command that's going to give you root privileges in your computer. If you don't run this program with sudo, you'll get an error message because most BPF programs can be loaded in the kernel only by a user who has root privileges.

When you run this program, you'll start to see our `Hello, BPF World!` message after a few seconds, even if you're not doing anything with your computer. This is because programs running behind the scenes in your computer might be executing other programs.

When you stop this program, the message will stop showing up in your terminal. BPF programs are unloaded from the VM as soon as the programs that load them terminate. In the coming chapters, we explore how to make BPF programs persistent, even after their loaders terminate, but we don't want to introduce too many concepts just yet. This is an important concept to keep in mind because in many situations, you'll want your BPF programs to run in the background, collecting data from your system, regardless of whether other processes are running.

Now that you've seen the basic structure for a BPF program, we can dive into which types of programs you can write, which will give you access to different subsystems within the Linux kernel.

BPF Program Types

Although there is no clear categorization within programs, you'll quickly realize that all the types covered in this section are divided in two categories, depending on what their main purpose is.

The first category is *tracing*. Many of the programs that you can write will help you better understand what's happening in your system. They give you direct information about the behavior of your system and the hardware it's running on. They can access memory regions related to specific programs, and extract execution traces from running processes. They also give you direct access to the resources allocated for each specific process, from file descriptors to CPU and memory usage.

The second category is *networking*. These types of programs allow you to inspect and manipulate the network traffic in your system. They let you filter packets coming from the network interface, or even reject those packets completely. Different types of programs can be attached to different stages of network processing within the kernel. This has advantages and disadvantages. For example, you can attach BPF programs to network events as soon as your network driver receives a packet, but this program will have access to less information about the packet, because the kernel doesn't have enough information to offer you yet. On the other end of the spectrum, you can attach BPF programs to network events immediately before they are passed to userspace. In this case, you'll have much more information about the packet, which will help you make better-informed decisions, but you'll need to pay the cost of completely processing the packet.

The list of program types that we show next is not divided into categories; we're introducing these types in the chronological order in which they were added to the kernel. We've moved the least used of these programs to the end of this section, and we'll focus for now on the ones that will be more useful for you. If you're curious about any program that we're not covering in detail here, you can learn more about all of them in man 2 bpf (*https://oreil.ly/qXl0F*).

Socket Filter Programs

BPF_PROG_TYPE_SOCKET_FILTER was the first program type to be added to the Linux kernel. When you attach a BPF program to a raw socket, you get access to all the packets processed by that socket. Socket filter programs don't allow you to modify the contents of those packets or to change the destination for those packets; they give you access to them for observability purposes only. The metadata that your program receives contains information related to the network stack such as the protocol type that's being used to deliver the packet.

We cover socket filtering and other network programs in more detail in Chapter 6.

Kprobe Programs

As you'll see in Chapter 4, in which we talk about tracing, kprobes are functions that you can attach dynamically to certain call points in the kernel. BPF kprobe program types allow you to use BPF programs as kprobe handlers. They are defined with the type BPF_PROG_TYPE_KPROBE. The BPF VM ensures that your kprobe programs are always safe to run, which is an advantage from traditional kprobe modules. You still need to remember that kprobes are not considered stable entry points in the kernel, so you'll need to ensure that your kprobe BPF programs are compatible with the specific kernel versions that you're using.

When you write a BPF program that's attached to a kprobe, you need to decide whether it will be executed as the first instruction in the function call or when the call completes. You need to declare this behavior in the section header of your BPF program. For example, if you want to inspect the arguments when the kernel invokes an exec syscall, you'll attach the program at the beginning of the call. In this case, you need to set the section header SEC("kprobe/sys_exec"). If you want to inspect the returned value of invoking an exec syscall, you need to set the section header SEC("kretprobe/sys_exec").

We talk a lot more about kprobes in later chapters of this book. They are a fundamental piece to understanding tracing with BPF.

Tracepoint Programs

This type of program allows you to attach BPF programs to the tracepoint handler provided by the kernel. Tracepoint programs are defined with the type BPF_PROG_TYPE_TRACEPOINT. As you'll see in Chapter 4, tracepoints are static marks in the kernel's codebase that allow you to inject arbitrary code for tracing and debugging purposes. They are less flexible than kprobes, because they need to be defined by the kernel beforehand, but they are guaranteed to be stable after their introduction in the kernel. This gives you a much higher level of predictability when you want to debug your system.

All tracepoints in your system are defined within the directory */sys/kernel/debug/tracing/events*. There you'll find each subsystem that includes any tracepoints and that you can attach a BPF program to. One interesting fact is that BPF declares its own tracepoints, so you can write BPF programs that inspect the behavior of other BPF programs. The BPF tracepoints are defined in */sys/kernel/debug/tracing/events/bpf*. There, for example, you can find the tracepoint definition for *bpf_prog_load*. This means you can write a BPF program that inspects when other BPF programs are loaded.

Like kprobes, tracepoints are another fundamental piece to understand tracing with BPF. We talk more about them in the coming chapters and show you how to write programs to take advantage of them.

XDP Programs

XDP programs allow you to write code that's executed very early on when a network packet arrives at the kernel. They are defined with the type BPF_PROG_TYPE_XDP. It exposes only a limited set of information from the packet given that the kernel has not had much time to process the information itself. Because the packet is executed early on, you have a much higher level of control over how to handle that packet.

XDP programs define several actions that you can control and that allow you to decide what to do with the packet. You can return XDP_PASS from your XDP program, which means that the packet should be passed to the next subsystem in the kernel. You can also return XDP_DROP, which means that the kernel should ignore this packet completely and do nothing else with it. You can also return XDP_TX, which means that the packet should be forwarded back to the network interface card (NIC) that received the packet in the first place.

This level of control opens the door to many interesting programs in the networking layer. XDP has become one of the main components in BPF, which is why we've included a specific chapter about it in this book. In Chapter 7, we discuss many powerful use cases for XDP, like implementing programs to protect your network against distributed denial-of-service (DDoS) attacks.

Perf Event Programs

These types of BPF programs allow you to attach your BPF code to *Perf events*. They are defined with the type BPF_PROG_TYPE_PERF_EVENT. Perf is an internal profiler in the kernel that emits performance data events for hardware and software. You can use it to monitor many things, from your computer's CPU to any software running on your system. When you attach a BPF program to Perf events, your code will be executed every time Perf generates data for you to analyze.

Cgroup Socket Programs

These types of programs allow you to attach BPF logic to control groups (cgroups). They are defined with the type BPF_PROG_TYPE_CGROUP_SKB. They allow cgroups to control network traffic within the processes that they contain. With these programs, you can decide what to do with a network packet before it's delivered to a process in the cgroup. Any packet that the kernel tries to deliver to any process in the same cgroup will pass through one of these filters. At the same time, you can decide what to do when a process in the cgroup sends a network packet through that interface.

As you can see, their behavior is similar to BPF_PROG_TYPE_SOCKET_FILTER programs. The main difference is that BPF_PROG_TYPE_CGROUP_SKB programs are attached to all processes within a cgroup, rather than specific processes; this behavior applies to current and future sockets created in the given cgroup. BPF programs attached to cgroups become useful in container environments where groups of processes are constrained by cgroups and where you can apply the same policies to all of them without having to identify each one independently. Cillium (*https://github.com/cilium/cilium*), a popular open source project that provides load balancing and security capabilities for Kubernetes, uses cgroup socket programs extensively to apply its policies in groups rather than in isolated containers.

Cgroup Open Socket Programs

These types of programs allow you to execute code when any process in a cgroup opens a network socket. This behavior is similar to the programs attached to cgroup socket buffers, but instead of giving you access to the packets as they come through the network, they allow you to control what happens when a process opens a new socket. They are defined with the type BPF_PROG_TYPE_CGROUP_SOCK. This is useful to provide security and access control over groups of programs that can open sockets without having to restrict capabilities per process individually.

Socket Option Programs

These types of programs allow you to modify socket connection options at runtime, while a packet transits through several stages in the kernel's networking stack. They are attached to cgroups, much like BPF_PROG_TYPE_CGROUP_SOCK and BPF_PROG_TYPE_CGROUP_SKB, but unlike those program types, they can be invoked several times during the connection's lifecycle. These programs are defined with the type BPF_PROG_TYPE_SOCK_OPS.

When you create a BPF program with this type, your function call receives an argument called op that represents the operation that the kernel is about to execute with the socket connection; therefore, you know at which point the program is invoked in the connection's lifecycle. With this information in hand, you can access data such as network IP addresses and connection ports, and you can modify the connection options to set timeouts and alter the round-trip delay time for a given packet.

For example, Facebook uses this to set short recovery time objectives (RTOs) for connections within the same datacenter. The RTO is the time that a system, or network connection in this case, is expected to be recovered after a failure. This objective also represents how long the system can be unavailable before suffering from unacceptable consequences. In Facebook's case, it assumes that machines in the same datacenter should have a short RTO, and Facebook modifies this threshold by using a BPF program.

Socket Map Programs

BPF_PROG_TYPE_SK_SKB programs give you access to socket maps and socket redirects. As you'll learn in the next chapter, socket maps allow you to keep references to several sockets. When you have these references, you can use special helpers to redirect an incoming packet from a socket to a different socket. This is interesting when you want to implement load-balancing capabilities with BPF. By keeping track of several sockets, you can forward network packets between them without leaving the kernel-space. Projects like Cillium and Facebook's Katran (*https://oreil.ly/wDtfR*) make extensive use of these types of programs for network traffic control.

Cgroup Device Programs

This type of program allows you to decide whether an operation within a cgroup can be executed for a given device. These programs are defined with the type BPF_PROG_TYPE_CGROUP_DEVICE. The first implementation of cgroups (v1) has a mechanism that allows you to set permissions for specific devices; however, the second iteration of cgroups lacks this feature. This type of program was introduced to supply that functionality. At the same time, being able to write a BPF program gives you more flexibility to set those permissions when you need them.

Socket Message Delivery Programs

These types of programs let you control whether a message sent to a socket should be delivered. They are defined with the type BPF_PROG_TYPE_SK_MSG. When the kernel creates a socket, it stores the socket in the aforementioned socket map. This map gives the kernel quick access to specific groups of sockets. When you attach a socket message BPF program to a socket map, all messages sent to those sockets will be filtered by the program before delivering them. Before filtering messages, the kernel copies the data in the message so that you can read it and decide what to do with it. These programs have two possible return values: SK_PASS and SK_DROP. You use the first one if you want the kernel to send the message to the socket, and you use the latter one if you want the kernel to ignore the message and not deliver it to the socket.

Raw Tracepoint Programs

We talked earlier about a type of program that accesses tracepoints in the kernel. The kernel developers added a new tracepoint program to address the need of accessing the tracepoint arguments in the raw format held by the kernel. This format gives you access to more detailed information about the task that the kernel is executing; however, it has a small performance overhead. Most of the time, you'll want to use regular tracepoints in your programs to avoid that performance overhead, but it's good to keep in mind that you can also access the raw arguments when needed by using raw tracepoints. These programs are defined with the type BPF_PROG_TYPE_RAW_TRACE POINT.

Cgroup Socket Address Programs

This type of program allows you to manipulate the IP addresses and port numbers that user-space programs are attached to when they are controlled by specific cgroups. There are use cases when your system uses several IP addresses when you want to ensure that a specific set of user-space programs use the same IP address and port. These BPF programs give you the flexibility to manipulate those bindings when you put those user-space programs in the same cgroup. This ensures that all incoming and outgoing connections from those applications use the IP and port that the BPF program provides. These programs are defined with the following type: BPF_PROG_TYPE_CGROUP_SOCK_ADDR.

Socket Reuseport Programs

SO_REUSEPORT is an option in the kernel that allows multiple processes in the same host to be bound to the same port. This option allows higher performance in accepted network connections when you want to distribute load across multiple threads.

The `BPF_PROG_TYPE_SK_REUSEPORT` program type allows you to write BPF programs that hook into the logic that the kernel uses to decide whether it's going to reuse a port. You can prevent programs from reusing the same port if your BPF program returns `SK_DROP`, and you also can inform the kernel to follow its own reuse routine when you return `SK_PASS` from these BPF programs.

Flow Dissection Programs

The flow dissector is a component of the kernel that keeps track of the different layers that a network packet needs to go through, from when it arrives to your system to when it's delivered to a user-space program. It allows you to control the flow of the packet using different classification methods. The built-in dissector in the kernel is called the *Flower classifier*, and it's used by firewalls and other filtering devices to decide what to do with specific packets.

`BPF_PROG_TYPE_FLOW_DISSECTOR` programs are designed to hook logic in the flow dissector path. They provide security guarantees that the built-in dissector cannot provide, such as ensuring that the program always terminates, which might not be guaranteed in the built-in dissector. These BPF programs can modify the flow that network packets follow within the kernel.

Other BPF Programs

We've talked about program types that we've seen used in different environments, but it's worth noting that there are a few other additional BPF program types that we haven't covered yet. These are programs that we mention only briefly here:

Traffic classifier programs
> `BPF_PROG_TYPE_SCHED_CLS` and `BPF_PROG_TYPE_SCHED_ACT` are two types of BPF programs that allow you to classify network traffic and modify some properties of the packets in the socket buffer.

Lightweight tunnel programs
> `BPF_PROG_TYPE_LWT_IN`, `BPF_PROG_TYPE_LWT_OUT`, `BPF_PROG_TYPE_LWT_XMIT` and `BPF_PROG_TYPE_LWT_SEG6LOCAL` are types of BPF programs that allow you to attach code to the kernel's lightweight tunnel infrastructure.

Infrared device programs
> `BPF_PROG_TYPE_LIRC_MODE2` programs allow you to attach BPF programs via connections to infrared devices, such as remote controllers, for fun.

These programs are specialized, and their usage has not been widely adopted for the community.

Next, we talk about how BPF guarantees that your programs won't cause a catastrophic failure in your system after the kernel loads them. This is an important topic because understanding how a program loads also influences how to write those programs.

The BPF Verifier

Allowing anyone to execute arbitrary code inside the Linux kernel always sounds like a terrible idea at first. The risk of running BPF programs in production systems would be too high if it weren't for the BPF verifier. In the words of Dave S. Miller, one of the kernel networking maintainers, "The only thing sitting between our eBPF programs and a deep dark chasm of destruction is the eBPF verifier."

Obviously, the BPF verifier is also a program running on your system, and it's the object of high scrutiny to ensure that it does its job correctly. In the past years, security researchers have discovered some vulnerabilities in the verifier that allowed attackers to access random memory in the kernel, even as unprivileged users. You can read more about vulnerabilities like that one in the Common Vulnerabilities and Exposures (CVE) catalog, a list of known security threads sponsored by the United States Department of Homeland Security. For example, CVE-2017-16995 describes how any user could read and write kernel memory and bypass the BPF verifier.

In this section we guide you through the measures that the verifier takes to prevent problems like the one just described.

The first check that the verifier performs is a static analysis of the code that the VM is going to load. The objective of this first check is to ensure that the program has an expected end. To do this, the verifier creates a direct acyclic graph (DAG) with the code. Each instruction that the verifier analyzes becomes a node in the graph, and each node is linked to the next instruction. After the verifier generates this graph, it performs a depth first search (DFS) to ensure that the program finishes and the code doesn't include dangerous paths. This means it will traverse each branch of the graph, all the way to the bottom of the branch, to guarantee that there are no recursive cycles.

These are the conditions why the verifier might reject your code during this first check:

- The program doesn't include control loops. To ensure that the program doesn't get stuck in an infinite loop, the verifier rejects any kind of control loop. There have been proposals to allow loops in BPF programs, but as of this writing, none of them has been adopted.

- The program doesn't try to execute more instructions than the maximum allowed by the kernel. At this time, the maximum number of instructions to execute is 4,096. This limitation is in place to prevent BPF from running forever. In

Chapter 3, we discuss how to nest different BPF programs to work around this limitation in a safe way.

- The program doesn't include any unreachable instruction, such as conditions or functions that are never executed. This prevents loading dead code in the VM, which would also delay the termination of the BPF program.

- The program doesn't try to jump outside its bounds.

The second check that the verifier performs is a dry run of the BPF program. This means that the verifier will try to analyze every instruction that the program is going to execute to ensure that it doesn't execute any invalid instruction. This execution also checks that all memory pointers are accessed and dereferenced correctly. Finally, the dry run informs the verifier about the control flows in the program to ensure that no matter which control path the program takes, it arrives to the BPF_EXIT instruction. To do this, the verifier keeps track of all visited branch paths in a stack, which it evaluates before taking a new path to ensure that it doesn't visit a specific path more than once. After these two checks pass, the verifier considers the program to be safe to execute.

The bpf syscall allows you to debug the verifier's checks if you're interested in seeing how your programs are analyzed. When you load a program with this syscall, you can set several attributes that will make the verifier print its operation log:

```
union bpf_attr attr = {
  .prog_type = type,
  .insns     = ptr_to_u64(insns),
  .insn_cnt  = insn_cnt,
  .license   = ptr_to_u64(license),
  .log_buf   = ptr_to_u64(bpf_log_buf),
  .log_size  = LOG_BUF_SIZE,
  .log_level = 1,
};

bpf(BPF_PROG_LOAD, &attr, sizeof(attr));
```

The log_level field tells the verifier whether to print any log. It will print its log when you set it to 1, and it won't print anything if you set it to 0. If you want to print the verifier log, you also need to provide a log buffer and its size. This buffer is a multiline string that you can print to inspect the decisions that the verifier took.

The BPF verifier plays a big role in keeping your system secure and available while you run arbitrary programs within the kernel, although it might be difficult to understand why it makes some decisions sometimes. Don't despair if you bump into verification issues trying to load your programs. During the rest of this book, we guide you through safe examples that will help you understand how to write your own programs in a secure way too.

The next section covers how BPF structures program information in memory. The way a program structured will help make clear how to access the BPF internals, helping you debug and understand how programs behave.

BPF Type Format

The BPF Type Format (BTF) is a collection of metadata structures that enhances the debug information for BPF programs, maps, and functions. BTF includes source information, so tools like BPFTool, which we talk about in Chapter 5, can show you a much richer interpretation of BPF data. This metadata is stored in the binary program under a special ".BFT" metadata section. BTF information is useful to make your programs easier to debug, but it increases the size of binary files significantly because it needs to keep track of type information for everything declared in your program. The BPF verifier also uses this information to ensure that the structure types defined by your program are correct.

BTF is used exclusively to annotate C types. BPF compilers like LLVM know how to include that information for you, so you don't need to go through the cumbersome task of adding that information to each structure. However, in some cases, the tool-chain still needs some annotations to enhance your programs. In later chapters we describe how those annotations come into play and how tools like BPFTool display this information.

BPF Tail Calls

BPF programs can call other BPF programs by using *tail calls*. This is a powerful feature because it allows you to assemble more complex programs by combining smaller BPF functions. Kernel versions prior to 5.2 have a hard limit on the number of machine instructions that a BPF program can generate. This limit was set to 4,096 to ensure that programs can terminate in a reasonable amount of time. However, as people built more complex BPF programs, they needed a way to extend the instruction limit imposed by the kernel, and this is where tail calls come into play. The instruction limit increases to one million instructions starting in version 5.2 of the kernel. Tail call nesting is also limited, to 32 calls in this case, which means that you can combine up to 32 programs in a chain to generate a more complex solution to your problems.

When you call a BPF program from another BPF program, the kernel resets the program context completely. It's important to keep this in mind because you'll probably need a way to share information between programs. The context object that each BPF program receives as its argument won't help us with this data sharing problem. In the next chapter, we talk about BPF maps as a way to share information between programs. There we also show you an example of how to use tail calls to jump from one BPF program to another.

Conclusion

In this chapter we guided you through the first code examples to understand BPF programs. We also described all the types of programs that you can write with BPF. Don't worry if some of the concepts presented here don't make sense yet; as we advance through the book, we show you more examples of those programs. We also covered the important verification steps that BPF takes to ensure that your programs are safe to run.

In the next chapter we dive a little bit more into those programs and show more examples. We also talk about how BPF programs communicate with their counterparts in user-space and how they share information.

BPF Maps

Message passing to invoke behavior in a program is a widely used technique in software engineering. A program can modify another program's behavior by sending messages; this also allows the exchange of information between those programs. One of the most fascinating aspects about BPF, is that the code running on the kernel and the program that loaded said code can communicate with each other at runtime using message passing.

In this chapter we cover how BPF programs and user-space programs can talk to one another. We describe the different channels of communication between the kernel and user-space, and how they store information. We also show you use cases for those channels and how to make the data in those channels persistent between programs initialization.

BPF maps are key/value stores that reside in the kernel. They can be accessed by any BPF program that knows about them. Programs that run in user-space can also access these maps by using file descriptors. You can store any kind of data in a map, as long as you specify the data size correctly beforehand. The kernel treats keys and values as binary blobs, and it doesn't care about what you keep in a map.

The BPF verifier includes several safeguards to ensure that the way you create and access maps is safe. We talk about these guarantees when we explain how to access data in these maps.

Creating BPF Maps

The most direct way to create a BPF map is by using the bpf syscall. When the first argument in the call is BPF_MAP_CREATE, you're telling the kernel that you want to create a new map. This call will return the file descriptor identifier associated with the map you just created. The second argument in the syscall is the configuration for this map:

```
union bpf_attr {
  struct {
    __u32 map_type;     /* one of the values from bpf_map_type */
    __u32 key_size;     /* size of the keys, in bytes */
    __u32 value_size;   /* size of the values, in bytes */
    __u32 max_entries;  /* maximum number of entries in the map */
    __u32 map_flags;    /* flags to modify how we create the map */
  };
}
```

The third argument in the syscall is the size of this configuration attribute.

For example, you can create a hash-table map to store unsigned integers as keys and values as follows:

```
union bpf_attr my_map {
  .map_type = BPF_MAP_TYPE_HASH,
  .key_size = sizeof(int),
  .value_size = sizeof(int),
  .max_entries = 100,
  .map_flags = BPF_F_NO_PREALLOC,
};

int fd = bpf(BPF_MAP_CREATE, &my_map, sizeof(my_map));
```

If the call fails, the kernel returns a value of -1. There might be three reasons why it fails. If one of the attributes is invalid, the kernel sets the errno variable to EINVAL. If the user executing the operation doesn't have enough privileges, the kernel sets the errno variable to EPERM. Finally, if there is not enough memory to store the map, the kernel sets the errno variable to ENOMEM.

In the following sections, we guide you through different examples to show you how to perform more advanced operations with BPF maps; let's begin with a more direct way to create any type of map.

ELF Conventions to Create BPF Maps

The kernel includes several conventions and helpers to generate and work with BPF maps. You'll probably find these conventions more frequently presented than direct syscall executions because they are more readable and easier to follow. Keep in mind that these conventions still use the bpf syscall to create the maps, even when run directly in the kernel, and you'll find using the syscall directly more useful if you don't know which kind of maps you're going to need beforehand.

The helper function `bpf_map_create` wraps the code you just saw to make it easier to initialize maps on demand. We can use it to create the previous map with only one line of code:

```
int fd;
fd = bpf_create_map(BPF_MAP_TYPE_HASH, sizeof(int), sizeof(int), 100,
    BPF_F_NO_PREALLOC);
```

If you know which kind of map you're going to need in your program, you can also predefine it. This is helpful to get more visibility in the maps your program is using beforehand:

```
struct bpf_map_def SEC("maps") my_map = {
    .type        = BPF_MAP_TYPE_HASH,
    .key_size    = sizeof(int),
    .value_size  = sizeof(int),
    .max_entries = 100,
    .map_flags   = BPF_F_NO_PREALLOC,
};
```

When you define a map in this way, you're using what's called a *section attribute*, in this case `SEC("maps")`. This macro tells the kernel that this structure is a BPF map and it should be created accordingly.

You might have noticed that we don't have the file descriptor identifier associated with the map in this new example. In this case, the kernel uses a global variable called `map_data` to store information about the maps in your program. This variable is an array of structures, and it's ordered by how you specified each map in your code. For example, if the previous map was the first one specified in your code, you'd get the file descriptor identifier from the first element in the array:

```
fd = map_data[0].fd;
```

You can also access the map's name and its definition from this structure; this information is sometimes useful for debugging and tracing purposes.

After you have initialized the map, you can begin sending messages between the kernel and user-space with them. Let's see now how to work with the data that these maps store.

Working with BFP Maps

Communication between the kernel and user-space is going to be a fundamental piece in every BPF program you write. The APIs to access maps differ when you're writing the code for the kernel than when you're writing the code for the user-space program. This section introduces the semantics and specific details of each implementation.

Updating Elements in a BPF Map

After creating any map, you'll probably want to populate it with information. The kernel helpers provide the function bpf_map_update_elem for this purpose. This function's signature is different if you load it from *bpf/bpf_helpers.h*, within the program running on the kernel, than if you load it from *tools/lib/bpf/bpf.h*, within the program running in user-space. This is because you can access maps directly when you're working in the kernel, but you reference them with file descriptors when you're working in user-space. Its behavior is also slightly different; the code running on the kernel can access the map in memory directly, and it will be able to update elements atomically in place. However, the code running in user-space has to send the message to the kernel, which copies the value supplied before updating the map; this makes the update operation not atomic. This function returns 0 when the operation succeeds, and it returns a negative number when it fails. In case of failure, the global variable errno is populated with the failure cause. We list failure cases later in this chapter with more context.

The bpf_map_update_elem function within the kernel takes four arguments. The first one is the pointer to the map we've already defined. The second one is a pointer to the key we want to update. Because the kernel doesn't know the type of key we're updating, this method is defined as an opaque pointer to void, which means we can pass any data. The third argument is the value we want to insert. This argument uses the same semantics as the key argument. We show some advanced examples of how to take advantage of opaque pointers throughout this book. You can use the fourth argument in this function to change the way the map is updated. This argument can take three values:

- If you pass 0, you're telling the kernel that you want to update the element if it exists or that it should create the element in the map if it doesn't exist.
- If you pass 1, you're telling the kernel to create the element only when it doesn't exist.
- If you pass 2, the kernel will update the element only when it exists.

These values are defined as constants that you can also use, instead of having to remember the integer semantics. The values are BPF_ANY for 0, BPF_NOEXIST for 1, and BPF_EXIST for 2.

Let's use the map we defined in the previous section to write some examples. In our first example, we add a new value to the map. Because the map is empty, we can assume that any update behavior is good for us:

```
int key, value, result;
key = 1, value = 1234;
```

```
result = bpf_map_update_elem(&my_map, &key, &value, BPF_ANY);
if (result == 0)
  printf("Map updated with new element\n");
else
  printf("Failed to update map with new value: %d (%s)\n",
      result, strerror(errno));
```

In this example we're using `strerror` to describe the error set in the `errno` variable. You can learn more about this function on the manual pages using `man strerror`.

Now let's see which result we get when we try to create an element with the same key:

```
int key, value, result;
key = 1, value = 5678;

result = bpf_map_update_elem(&my_map, &key, &value, BPF_NOEXIST);
if (result == 0)
  printf("Map updated with new element\n");
else
  printf("Failed to update map with new value: %d (%s)\n",
      result, strerror(errno));
```

Because we have already created an element with key 1 in our map, the result from calling `bpf_map_update_elem` will be `-1`, and the `errno` value will be EEXIST. This program will print the following on the screen:

```
Failed to update map with new value: -1 (File exists)
```

Similarly, let's change this program to try to update an element that doesn't exist yet:

```
int key, value, result;
key = 1234, value = 5678;

result = bpf_map_update_elem(&my_map, &key, &value, BPF_EXIST);
if (result == 0)
  printf("Map updated with new element\n");
else
  printf("Failed to update map with new value: %d (%s)\n",
      result, strerror(errno));
```

With the flag `BPF_EXIST`, the result of this operation is going to be `-1` again. The kernel will set the `errno` variable to ENOENT, and the program will print the following:

```
Failed to update map with new value: -1 (No such file or directory)
```

These examples show how you can update maps from within the kernel program. You can also update maps from within user-space programs. The helpers to do this are similar to the ones we just saw; the only difference is that they use the file descriptor to access the map, rather than using the pointer to the map directly. As you remember, user-space programs always access maps using file descriptors. So in our examples, we'd replace the argument `my_map` with the global file descriptor identifier `map_data[0].fd`. Here is what the original code looks like in this case:

```
int key, value, result;
key = 1, value = 1234;

result = bpf_map_update_elem(map_data[0].fd, &key, &value, BPF_ANY);
if (result == 0)
  printf("Map updated with new element\n");
else
  printf("Failed to update map with new value: %d (%s)\n",
      result, strerror(errno));
```

Although the type of information that you can store in a map is directly related to the type of map that you're working with, the method to populate the information will remain the same, as you saw in this previous example. We discuss the types of keys and values accepted for each type of map later; let's first see how to manipulate the store data.

Reading Elements from a BPF Map

Now that we've populated our map with new elements, we can begin reading them from other points in our code. The reading API will look familiar after learning about bpf_map_update_element.

BPF also provides two different helpers to read from a map depending on where your code is running. Both helpers are called bpf_map_lookup_elem. Like the update helpers, they differ in their first argument; the kernel method takes a reference to the map, whereas the user-space helper takes the map's file descriptor identifier as its first argument. Both methods return an integer to represent whether the operation failed or succeeded, just like the update helpers. The third argument in these helpers is a pointer to the variable in your code that's going to store the value read from the map. We present two examples based on the code you saw in the previous section.

The first example reads the value inserted in the map when the BPF program is running on the kernel:

```
int key, value, result; // value is going to store the expected element's value
key = 1;

result = bpf_map_lookup_elem(&my_map, &key, &value);
if (result == 0)
  printf("Value read from the map: '%d'\n", value);
else
  printf("Failed to read value from the map: %d (%s)\n",
      result, strerror(errno));
```

If the key we were trying to read, bpf_map_lookup_elem, returned a negative number, it would set the error in the errno variable. For example, if we had not inserted the value before trying to read it, the kernel would have returned the "not found" error ENOENT.

This second example is similar to the one you just saw, but this time we're reading the map from the program running in user-space:

```
int key, value, result; // value is going to store the expected element's value
key = 1;

result = bpf_map_lookup_elem(map_data[0].fd, &key, &value);
if (result == 0)
  printf("Value read from the map: '%d'\n", value);
else
  printf("Failed to read value from the map: %d (%s)\n",
      result, strerror(errno));
```

As you can see, we've replaced the first argument in bpf_map_lookup_elem with the map's file descriptor identifier. The helper behavior is the same as the previous example.

That's all we need to be able to access information within a BPF map. We examine how this has been streamlined by different toolkits to make accessing data even simpler in later chapters. Let's talk about deleting data from maps next.

Removing an Element from a BPF Map

The third operation we can execute on maps is to remove elements. Like with writing and reading elements, BPF gives us two different helpers to remove elements, both called bpf_map_delete_element. Like in the previous examples, these helpers use the direct reference to the map when you use them in the program running on the kernel, and they use the map's file descriptor identifier when you use them in the program running on user-space.

The first example deletes the value inserted in the map when the BPF program is running on the kernel:

```
int key, result;
key = 1;

result = bpf_map_delete_element(&my_map, &key);
if (result == 0)
  printf("Element deleted from the map\n");
else
  printf("Failed to delete element from the map: %d (%s)\n",
      result, strerror(errno));
```

If the element that you're trying to delete doesn't exist, the kernel returns a negative number. In that case, it also populates the errno variable with the "not found" error ENOENT.

This second example deletes the value when the BPF program is running on user-space:

```
int key, result;
key = 1;

result = bpf_map_delete_element(map_data[0].fd, &key);
if (result == 0)
  printf("Element deleted from the map\n");
else
  printf("Failed to delete element from the map: %d (%s)\n",
      result, strerror(errno));
```

You can see that we've changed the first argument again to use the file descriptor identifier. Its behavior is going to be consistent with the kernel's helper.

This concludes what could be considered the create/read/update/delete (CRUD) operations of the BPF map. The kernel exposes some additional functions to help you with other common operations; we'll talk about some of them in the next two sections.

Iterating Over Elements in a BPF Map

The final operation we look at in this section can help you to find arbitrary elements in a BPF program. There will be occasions when you don't know exactly the key for the element you're looking for or you just want to see what's inside a map. BPF provides an instruction for this called bpf_map_get_next_key. Unlike the helpers you've seen up to now, this instruction is available only for programs running on user-space.

This helper gives you a deterministic way to iterate over the elements on a map, but its behavior is less intuitive than iterators in most programming languages. It takes three arguments. The first one is the map's file descriptor identifier, like the other user-space helpers you've already seen. The next two arguments are where it becomes tricky. According to the official documentation, the second argument, key, is the identifier you're looking for, and the third one, next_key, is the next key in the map. We prefer to call the first argument lookup_key—it's going to become apparent why in a second. When you call this helper, BPF tries to find the element in this map with the key that you're passing as the lookup key; then, it sets the next_key argument with the adjacent key in the map. So if you want to know which key comes after key 1, you need to set 1 as your lookup key, and if the map has an adjacent key to this one, BPF will set it as the value for the next_key argument.

Before seeing how bpf_map_get_next_key works in an example, let's add a few more elements to our map:

```
int new_key, new_value, it;

for (it = 2; it < 6 ; it++) {
```

```
    new_key = it;
    new_value = 1234 + it;
    bpf_map_update_elem(map_data[0].fd, &new_key, &new_value, BPF_NOEXIST);
}
```

If you want to print all of the values in the map, you can use bpf_map_get_next_key with a lookup key that doesn't exist in the map. This forces BPF to start from the beginning of the map:

```
int next_key, lookup_key;
lookup_key = -1;

while(bpf_map_get_next_key(map_data[0].fd, &lookup_key, &next_key) == 0) {
    printf("The next key in the map is: '%d'\n", next_key);
    lookup_key = next_key;
}
```

This code prints something like this:

```
The next key in the map is: '1'
The next key in the map is: '2'
The next key in the map is: '3'
The next key in the map is: '4'
The next key in the map is: '5'
```

You can see that we're assigning the next key to lookup_key at the end of the loop; that way, we continue iterating over the map until we reach the end. When bpf_map_get_next_key arrives at the end of the map, the value returned is a negative number, and the errno variable is set to ENOENT. This will abort the loop execution.

As you can imagine, bpf_map_get_next_key can look up keys starting at any point in the map; you don't need to start at the beginning of the map if you want only the next key for another specific key.

The tricks that bpf_map_get_next_key can play on you don't end here; there is another behavior that you need to be aware of. Many programming languages copy the values in a map before iterating over its elements. This prevents unknown behaviors if some other code in your program decides to mutate the map. This is especially dangerous if that code deletes elements from the map. BPF doesn't copy the values in a map before looping over them with bpf_map_get_next_key. If another part of your program deletes an element from the map while you're looping over the values, bpf_map_get_next_key will start over when it tries to find the next value for the element's key that was removed. Let's see this with an example:

```
int next_key, lookup_key;
lookup_key = -1;

while(bpf_map_get_next_key(map_data[0].fd, &lookup_key, &next_key) == 0) {
    printf("The next key in the map is: '%d'\n", next_key);
    if (next_key == 2) {
```

```
    printf("Deleting key '2'\n");
    bpf_map_delete_element(map_data[0].fd &next_key);
  }
  lookup_key = next_key;
}
```

This program prints the next output:

```
The next key in the map is: '1'
The next key in the map is: '2'
Deleteing key '2'
The next key in the map is: '1'
The next key in the map is: '3'
The next key in the map is: '4'
The next key in the map is: '5'
```

This behavior is not very intuitive, so keep it in mind when you use bpf_map_get_next_key.

Because most of the map types that we cover in this chapter behave like arrays, iterating over them is going to be a key operation when you want to access the information that they store. However, there are additional functions to access data, as you'll see next.

Looking Up and Deleting Elements

Another interesting function that the kernel exposes to work with maps is bpf_map_lookup_and_delete_elem. This function searches for a given key in the map and deletes the element from it. At the same time, it writes the value of the element in a variable for your program to use. This function comes in handy when you use queue and stack maps, which we describe in the next section. However, it's not restricted for use only with those types of maps. Let's see an example of how to use it with the map we've been using in our previous examples:

```
int key, value, result, it;
key = 1;

for (it = 0; it < 2; it++) {
  result = bpf_map_lookup_and_delete_element(map_data[0].fd, &key, &value);
  if (result == 0)
    printf("Value read from the map: '%d'\n", value);
  else
    printf("Failed to read value from the map: %d (%s)\n",
        result, strerror(errno));
}
```

In this example, we try to fetch the same element from the map twice. In the first iteration, this code will print the value of the element in the map. However, because we're using bpf_map_lookup_and_delete_element, this first iteration will also delete the element from the map. The second time the loop tries to fetch the element, this code will fail, and it will populate the `errno` variable with the "not found" error `ENOENT`.

Until now, we haven't paid much attention to what happens when concurrent operations try to access the same piece of information within a BPF map. Let's talk about this next.

Concurrent Access to Map Elements

One of the challenges of working with BPF maps is that many programs can access the same maps concurrently. This can introduce race conditions in our BPF programs, and make accessing resources in maps unpredictable. To prevent race conditions, BPF introduced the concept of BPF spin locks, which allow you to lock access to a map's element while you're operating on it. Spin locks work only on array, hash, and cgroup storage maps.

There are two BPF helper functions to work with spin locks: `bpf_spin_lock` locks an element, and `bpf_spin_unlock` unlocks that element. These helpers work with a structure that acts as a semaphone to access an element that includes this semaphore. When the semaphore is locked, other programs cannot access the element's value, and they wait until the semaphore is unlocked. At the same time, BPF spin locks introduce a new flag that user-space programs can use to change the state of that lock; that flag is called `BPF_F_LOCK`.

The first thing we need to do to work with spin locks is create the element that we want to lock access to and then add our semaphore:

```
struct concurrent_element {
  struct bpf_spin_lock semaphore;
  int count;
}
```

We'll store this structure in our BPF map, and we'll use the semaphore within the element to prevent undesired access to it. Now, we can declare the map that's going to hold these elements. This map must be annotated with BPF Type Format (BTF) so the verifier knows how to intepret the structure. The type format gives the kernel and other tools a much richer understanding of BPF data structures by adding debug information to binary objects. Because this code will run within the kernel, we can use the kernel macros that `libbpf` provides to annotate this concurrent map:

```
struct bpf_map_def SEC("maps") concurrent_map = {
    .type        = BPF_MAP_TYPE_HASH,
    .key_size    = sizeof(int),
    .value_size  = sizeof(struct concurrent_element),
    .max_entries = 100,
};

BPF_ANNOTATE_KV_PAIR(concurrent_map, int, struct concurrent_element);
```

Within a BPF program we can use the two locking helpers to protect from race conditions on those elements. Even though the semaphore is locked, our program is guaranteed to be able to modify the element's value safely:

```
int bpf_program(struct pt_regs *ctx) {
    int key = 0;
    struct concurrent_element init_value = {};
    struct concurrent_element *read_value;

    bpf_map_create_elem(&concurrent_map, &key, &init_value, BPF_NOEXIST);

    read_value = bpf_map_lookup_elem(&concurrent_map, &key);
    bpf_spin_lock(&read_value->semaphore);
    read_value->count += 100;
    bpf_spin_unlock(&read_value->semaphore);
}
```

This example initializes our concurrent map with a new entry that can lock access to its value. Then, it fetches that value from the map and locks its semaphore so that it can hold the count value, preventing data races. When it's done using the value, it releases the lock so other maps can access the element safely.

From user-space, we can hold the reference to an element in our concurrent map by using the flag BPF_F_LOCK. You can use this flag with the bpf_map_update_elem and bpf_map_lookup_elem_flags helper functions. This flag allows you to update elements in place without having to worry about data races.

 BPF_F_LOCK has a slightly different behavior when updating hash map and updating array and cgroup storage maps. With the latter two, the updates happen in place, and the elements that you're updating must exist in the map before executing the update. In the case of hash maps, if the element doesn't exist already, the program locks the bucket in the map for the element and inserts a new element.

Spin locks are not always necessary. You don't need them if you're only aggregating values in a map. However, they are useful if you want to ensure that concurrent programs don't change elements in a map when you're performing several operations on them, preserving atomicity.

In this section you've seen the possible operations you can do with BPF maps; however, we've worked with only one type of map so far. BPF includes many more map types that you can use in different situations. We explain all types of maps that BPF defines and show you specific examples on how to use them for different situations.

Types of BPF Maps

The Linux documentation (*https://oreil.ly/XfoqK*) defines maps as generic data structures where you can store different types of data. Over the years, the kernel developers have added many specialized data structures that are more efficient in specific use cases. This section explores each type of map and how you can use them.

Hash-Table Maps

Hash-table maps were the first generic map added to BPF. They are defined with the type `BPF_MAP_TYPE_HASH`. Their implementation and usage are similar to other hash tables you might be familiar with. You can use keys and values of any size; the kernel takes care of allocating and freeing them for you as needed. When you use `bpf_map_update_elem` on a hash-table map, the kernel replaces the elements atomically.

Hash-table maps are optimized to be very fast at lookup; they are useful for keeping structured data that's read frequently. Let's see an example program that uses them to keep track of network IPs and their rate limits:

```
#define IPV4_FAMILY 1
struct ip_key {
  union {
    __u32 v4_addr;
    __u8 v6_addr[16];
  };
  __u8 family;
};

struct bpf_map_def SEC("maps") counters = {
    .type        = BPF_MAP_TYPE_HASH,
    .key_size    = sizeof(struct ip_key),
    .value_size  = sizeof(uint64_t),
    .max_entries = 100,
    .map_flags   = BPF_F_NO_PREALLOC
};
```

In this code we've declared a structured key, and we're going to use it to keep information about IP addresses. We define the map that our program will use to keep track of rate limits. You can see that we're using the IP addresses as keys in this map. The values are going to be the number of times that our BPF program receives a network packet from a specific IP address.

Let's write a small code snippet that updates those counters in the kernel:

```
uint64_t update_counter(uint32_t ipv4) {
  uint64_t value;
  struct ip_key key = {};
  key.v4_addr = ip4;
```

```
    key.family = IPV4_FAMILY;

    bpf_map_lookup_elem(counters, &key, &value);
    (*value) += 1;
}
```

This function takes an IP address extracted from a network packet and performs the map lookup with the compound key that we're declaring. In this case, we're assuming that we've previously initialized the counter with a zero value; otherwise, the bpf_map_lookup_elem call would return a negative number.

Array Maps

Array maps were the second type of BPF map added to the kernel. They are defined with the type BPF_MAP_TYPE_ARRAY. When you initialize an array map, all of its elements are preallocated in memory and set to their zero value. Because these maps are backed by a slice of elements, the keys are indexes in the array, and their size must be exactly four bytes.

A disadvantage of using array maps is that the elements in the map cannot be removed and you cannot make the array smaller than it is. If you try to use map_delete_elem on an array map, the call will fail, and you'll get an error EINVAL as a result.

Array maps are commonly used to store information that can change in value, but it's usually fixed in behavior. People use them to store global variables with a predefined assignment rule. Because you cannot remove elements, you can assume that the element in a specific position always represents the same element.

Something else to keep in mind is that map_update_elem is not atomic, like you saw with hash-table maps. The same program can read different values from the same position at the same time if there is an update in process. If you're storing counters in an array map, you can use the kernel's built-in function __sync_fetch_and_add to perform atomic operations on the map's values.

Program Array Maps

Program array maps were the first specialized map added to the kernel. They are defined with the type BPF_MAP_TYPE_PROG_ARRAY. You can use this type of map to store references to BPF programs using their file descriptor identifiers. In conjunction with the helper bpf_tail_call, this map allows you to jump between programs, bypassing the maximum instruction limit of single BPF programs and reducing implementation complexity.

There are a few things you need to consider when you use this specialized map. The first aspect to remember is that both key and value sizes must be four bytes. The second aspect to remember is that when you jump to a new program, the new program will reuse the same memory stack, so your program doesn't consume all the available memory. Finally, if you try to jump to a program that doesn't exist in the map, the tail call will fail, and the current program will continue its execution.

Let's dive into a detailed example to understand how to use this type of map better:

```
struct bpf_map_def SEC("maps") programs = {
  .type = BPF_MAP_TYPE_PROG_ARRAY,
  .key_size = 4,
  .value_size = 4,
  .max_entries = 1024,
};
```

First, we need to declare our new program map (as we mentioned earlier, the key and value sizes are always four bytes):

```
int key = 1;
struct bpf_insn prog[] = {
  BPF_MOV64_IMM(BPF_REG_0, 0), // assign r0 = 0
  BPF_EXIT_INSN(),  // return r0
};

prog_fd = bpf_prog_load(BPF_PROG_TYPE_KPROBE, prog, sizeof(prog), "GPL");
bpf_map_update_elem(&programs, &key, &prog_fd, BPF_ANY);
```

We need to declare the program that we're going to jump to. In this case, we're writing a BPF program, and its only purpose is to return 0. We use `bpf_prog_load` to load it in the kernel, and then we add its file descriptor identifier to our program map.

Now that we have that program stored, we can write another BPF program that will jump to it. BPF programs can jump to other programs only if they are of the same type; in this case, we're attaching the program to a kprobe trace, like we saw in Chapter 2:

```
SEC("kprobe/seccomp_phase1")
int bpf_kprobe_program(struct pt_regs *ctx) {
  int key = 1;
  /* dispatch into next BPF program */
  bpf_tail_call(ctx, &programs, &key);

  /* fall through when the program descriptor is not in the map */
  char fmt[] = "missing program in prog_array map\n";
  bpf_trace_printk(fmt, sizeof(fmt));
  return 0;
}
```

With `bpf_tail_call` and `BPF_MAP_TYPE_PROG_ARRAY`, you can chain up to 32 nested calls. This is an explicit limit to prevent infinite loops and memory exhaustion.

Perf Events Array Maps

These types of maps store `perf_events` data in a buffer ring that communicates between BPF programs and user-space programs in real time. They are defined with the type `BPF_MAP_TYPE_PERF_EVENT_ARRAY`. They are designed to forward events that the kernel's tracing tools emit to user-space programs for further processing. This is one of the most interesting types of maps and is the base for many observability tools that we'll talk about in the next chapters. The user-space program acts as a listener that waits for events coming from the kernel, so you need to make sure that your code starts listening before the BPF program in the kernel is initialized.

Let's see an example of how we can trace all the programs that our computer executes. Before jumping into the BPF program code, we need to declare the event structure that we're going to send from the kernel to user-space:

```
struct data_t {
  u32 pid;
  char program_name[16];
};
```

Now, we need to create the map that's going to send the events to user-space:

```
struct bpf_map_def SEC("maps") events = {
  .type = BPF_MAP_TYPE_PERF_EVENT_ARRAY,
  .key_size = sizeof(int),
  .value_size = sizeof(u32),
  .max_entries = 2,
};
```

After we have our data type and map declared, we can create the BPF program that captures the data and sends it to user-space:

```
SEC("kprobe/sys_exec")
int bpf_capture_exec(struct pt_regs *ctx) {
  data_t data;
  // bpf_get_current_pid_tgid returns the current process identifier
  data.pid = bpf_get_current_pid_tgid() >> 32;
  // bpf_get_current_comm loads the current executable name
  bpf_get_current_comm(&data.program_name, sizeof(data.program_name));
  bpf_perf_event_output(ctx, &events, 0, &data, sizeof(data));
  return 0;
}
```

In this snippet, we're using `bpf_perf_event_output` to append the data to the map. Because this is a real-time buffer, you don't need worry about keys for the elements in the map; the kernel takes care of adding the new element to the map and flushing it after the user-space program processes it.

In Chapter 4 we talk about more advanced usages for these types of maps, and we present examples of processing programs in user-space.

Per-CPU Hash Maps

This type of map is a refined version of `BPF_MAP_TYPE_HASH`. These maps are defined with the type `BPF_MAP_TYPE_PERCPU_HASH`. When you allocate one of these maps, each CPU sees its own isolated version of the map, which makes it much more efficient for high-performant lookups and aggregations. This type of map is useful if your BPF program collects metrics and aggregates them in hash-table maps.

Per-CPU Array Maps

This type of map is also a refined version of `BPF_MAP_TYPE_ARRAY`. They are defined with the type `BPF_MAP_TYPE_PERCPU_ARRAY`. Just like the previous map, when you allocate one of these maps, each CPU sees its own isolated version of the map, which makes it much more efficient for high-performant lookups and aggregations.

Stack Trace Maps

This type of map stores stack traces from the running process. They are defined with the type `BPF_MAP_TYPE_STACK_TRACE`. Along with this map, the kernel developers already added the helper `bpf_get_stackid` to help you populate this map with stack traces. This helper takes the map as an argument and a series of flags so that you can specify whether you want traces only from the kernel, only from user-space, or both. The helper returns the key associated with the element added to the map.

Cgroup Array Maps

This type of map stores references to cgroups. Cgroup array maps are defined with the type `BPF_MAP_TYPE_CGROUP_ARRAY`. In essence, their behavior is similar to `BPF_MAP_TYPE_PROG_ARRAY`, but they store file descriptor identifiers that point to cgroups.

This map is useful when you want to share cgroup references between BPF maps for controlling traffic, debugging, and testing. Let's see an example of how to populate this map. We start with the map definition:

```
struct bpf_map_def SEC("maps") cgroups_map = {
  .type = BPF_MAP_TYPE_CGROUP_ARRAY,
  .key_size = sizeof(uint32_t),
  .value_size = sizeof(uint32_t),
  .max_entries = 1,
};
```

We can retrieve a cgroup's file descriptor by opening the file containing its information. We're going to open the cgroup that controls the base CPU shares for Docker containers and store that cgroup in our map:

```
int cgroup_fd, key = 0;
cgroup_fd = open("/sys/fs/cgroup/cpu/docker/cpu.shares", O_RDONLY);

bpf_update_elem(&cgroups_map, &key, &cgroup_fd, 0);
```

LRU Hash and Per-CPU Hash Maps

These two types of map are hash-table maps, like the ones you saw earlier, but they also implement an internal LRU cache. LRU stands for least recently used, which means that if the map is full, these maps will erase elements that are not used frequently to make room for new elements in the map. Therefore, you can use these maps to insert elements beyond the maximum limit, as long as you don't mind loosing elements that have not been used recently. They are defined with the types BPF_MAP_TYPE_LRU_HASH and BPF_MAP_TYPE_LRU_PERCPU_HASH.

The per cpu version of this map is slightly different than the other per cpu maps you saw earlier. This map keeps only one hash table to store all the elements in the map, and it uses different LRU caches per CPU, that way, it ensures that the most used elements in each CPU remain in the map.

LPM Trie Maps

LPM trie maps are types of map that use longest prefix match (LPM) to look up elements in the map. LPM is an algorithm that selects the element in a tree that matches with the longest lookup key from any other match in the tree. This algorithm is used in routers and other devices that keep traffic forwarding tables to match IP addresses with specific routes. These maps are defined with the type BPF_MAP_TYPE_LPM_TRIE.

These maps require their key sizes to be multiples of eight and in a range from 8 to 2,048. If you don't want to implement your own key, the kernel provides a struct that you can use for these keys called bpf_lpm_trie_key.

In this next example, we add two forwarding routes to the map and try to match an IP address to the correct route. First we need to create the map:

```
struct bpf_map_def SEC("maps") routing_map = {
  .type = BPF_MAP_TYPE_LPM_TRIE,
  .key_size = 8,
  .value_size = sizeof(uint64_t),
  .max_entries = 10000,
  .map_flags = BPF_F_NO_PREALLOC,
};
```

We're going to populate this map with three forwarding routes: 192.168.0.0/16, 192.168.0.0/24, and 192.168.1.0/24:

```
uint64_t value_1 = 1;
struct bpf_lpm_trie_key route_1 = {.data = {192, 168, 0, 0}, .prefixlen = 16};
uint64_t value_2 = 2;
```

```
struct bpf_lpm_trie_key route_2 = {.data = {192, 168, 0, 0}, .prefixlen = 24};
uint64_t value_3 = 3;
struct bpf_lpm_trie_key route_3 = {.data = {192, 168, 1, 0}, .prefixlen = 24};

bpf_map_update_elem(&routing_map, &route_1, &value_1, BPF_ANY);
bpf_map_update_elem(&routing_map, &route_2, &value_2, BPF_ANY);
bpf_map_update_elem(&routing_map, &route_3, &value_3, BPF_ANY);
```

Now, we use the same key structure to look up the correct match for the IP 192.168.1.1/32:

```
uint64_t result;
struct bpf_lpm_trie_key lookup = {.data = {192, 168, 1, 1}, .prefixlen = 32};

int ret = bpf_map_lookup_elem(&routing_map, &lookup, &result);
if (ret == 0)
  printf("Value read from the map: '%d'\n", result);
```

In this example, both 192.168.0.0/24 and 192.168.1.0/24 could match the lookup IP because it's within both ranges. However, because this map uses the LPM algorithm, the result will be populated with the value for the key 192.168.1.0/24.

Array of Maps and Hash of Maps

BPF_MAP_TYPE_ARRAY_OF_MAPS and BPF_MAP_TYPE_HASH_OF_MAPS are two types of maps that store references to other maps. They support only one level of indirection, so you cannot use them to store maps of maps of maps, and so on. This ensures that you don't consume all of the memory by accidentally storing infinite chained maps.

These types of maps are useful when you want to be able to replace entire maps at runtime. You can create full-state snapshots if all of your maps are children of a global map. The kernel ensures that any update operation in the parent map waits until all the references to old children maps are dropped before completing the operation.

Device Map Maps

This specialized type of map stores references to network devices. These maps are defined with the type BPF_MAP_TYPE_DEVMAP. They are useful for network applications that want to manipulate traffic at the kernel level. You can build a virtual map of ports that point to specific network devices and then redirect packets by using the helper bpf_redirect_map.

CPU Map Maps

BPF_MAP_TYPE_CPUMAP is another type of map that allows you to forward network traffic. In this case, the map stores references to different CPUs in your host. Like the previous type of map, you can use it with the bpf_redirect_map helper to redirect packets. However, this map sends packets to a different CPU. This allows you to assign specific CPUs to network stacks for scalability and isolation purposes.

Open Socket Maps

BPF_MAP_TYPE_XSKMAP is a type of map that stores references to open sockets. Like the previous maps, these maps are useful for forwarding packets, between sockets in this case.

Socket Array and Hash Maps

BPF_MAP_TYPE_SOCKMAP and BPF_MAP_TYPE_SOCKHASH are two specialized maps that store references to open sockets in the kernel. Like the previous maps, this type of maps is used in conjunction with the helper bpf_redirect_map to forward socket buffers from the current XDP program to a different socket.

Their main difference is that one of them uses an array to store the sockets and the other one uses a hash table. The advantage of using a hash table is that you can access a socket directly by its key without the need to traverse the full map to find it. Each socket in the kernel is identified by a five-tuple key. These five tuples include the necessary information to establish bidirectional network connections. You can use this key as the lookup key in your map when you use the hash-table version of this map.

Cgroup Storage and Per-CPU Storage Maps

These two types of maps were introduced to help developers work with BPF programs attached to cgroups. As you saw in Chapter 2, you can attach and detach BPF programs from control groups and isolate their runtime to specific cgroups with BPF_PROG_TYPE_CGROUP_SKB. These two maps are defined with the types BPF_MAP_TYPE_CGROUP_STORAGE and BPF_MAP_TYPE_PERCPU_CGROUP_STORAGE.

These types of maps are similar to hash-table maps from the developer point of view. The kernel provides a structure helper to generate keys for this map, bpf_cgroup_storage_key, which includes information about the cgroup node identifier and the attachment type. You can add any value you want to this map; its access will be restricted to the BPF program inside the attached cgroup.

There are two limitations with these maps. The first is that you cannot create new elements in the map from user-space. The BPF program in the kernel can create elements with bpf_map_update_elem, but if you use this method from user-space and the key doesn't exist already, bpf_map_update_elem will fail, and errno will be set to ENOENT. The second limitation is that you cannot remove elements from this map. bpf_map_delete_elem always fails and sets errno to EINVAL.

The main difference between these two types of maps, as you saw with other similar maps earlier, is that BPF_MAP_TYPE_PERCPU_CGROUP_STORAGE keeps a different hash table per CPU.

Reuseport Socket Maps

This specialized type of map stores references to sockets that can be reused by an open port in the system. They are defined with the type BPF_MAP_TYPE_REUSE PORT_SOCKARRAY. These maps are mainly used with BPF_PROG_TYPE_SK_REUSEPORT program types. Combined, they give you control to decide how to filter and serve incoming packets from the network device. For example, you can decide which packets go to which socket, even though both sockets are attached to the same port.

Queue Maps

Queue maps use a first-in, first-out (FIFO) storage to keep the elements in the map. They are defined with the type BPF_MAP_TYPE_QUEUE. FIFO means that when you fetch an element from the map, the result is going to be the element that has been in the map for the longest time.

The bpf map helpers work in a predictable way for this data structure. When you use bpf_map_lookup_elem, this map always looks for the oldest element in the map. When you use bpf_map_update_elem, this map always appends the element to the end of the queue, so you'll need to read the rest elements in the map before being able to fetch this element. You can also use the helper bpf_map_lookup_and_delete to fetch the older element and remove it from the map in an atomic way. This map doesn't support the helpers bpf_map_delete_elem and bpf_map_get_next_key. If you try to use them, they will fail and set the errno variable to EINVAL as a result.

Something else that you need to keep in mind about these types of map is that they don't use the map keys for lookups, and the key size must always be 0 when you initialize these maps. When you push elements to these maps, the key must be a null value.

Let's see an example of how to use this type of map:

```
struct bpf_map_def SEC("maps") queue_map = {
  .type = BPF_MAP_TYPE_QUEUE,
  .key_size = 0,
  .value_size = sizeof(int),
  .max_entries = 100,
  .map_flags = 0,
};
```

Let's insert several elements in this map and retrieve them in the same order in which we inserted them:

```
  int i;
  for (i = 0; i < 5; i++)
    bpf_map_update_elem(&queue_map, NULL, &i, BPF_ANY);

  int value;
  for (i = 0; i < 5; i++) {
    bpf_map_lookup_and_delete(&queue_map, NULL, &value);
    printf("Value read from the map: '%d'\n", value);
  }
```

This program prints the following:

```
Value read from the map: '0'
Value read from the map: '1'
Value read from the map: '2'
Value read from the map: '3'
Value read from the map: '4'
```

If we try to pop a new element from the map, bpf_map_lookup_and_delete will return a negative number, and the errno variable will be set to ENOENT.

Stack Maps

Stack maps use a last-in, first-out (LIFO) storage to keep the elements in the map. They are defined with the type BPF_MAP_TYPE_STACK. LIFO means that when you fetch an element from the map, the result is going to be the element that was added to the map most recently.

The bpf map helpers also work in a predictable way for this data structure. When you use bpf_map_lookup_elem, this map always looks for the newest element in the map. When you use bpf_map_update_elem, this map always appends the element to the top of the stack, so it's the first one to fetch. You can also use the helper bpf_map_lookup_and_delete to fetch the newest element and remove it from the map in an atomic way. This map doesn't support the helpers bpf_map_delete_elem and bpf_map_get_next_key. If you try to use them, they will always fail and set the errno variable to EINVAL as a result.

Let's see an example of how to use this map:

```
struct bpf_map_def SEC("maps") stack_map = {
  .type = BPF_MAP_TYPE_STACK,
  .key_size = 0,
  .value_size = sizeof(int),
  .max_entries = 100,
  .map_flags = 0,
};
```

Let's insert several elements in this map and retrieve them in the same order in which we inserted them:

```
int i;
for (i = 0; i < 5; i++)
  bpf_map_update_elem(&stack_map, NULL, &i, BPF_ANY);

int value;
for (i = 0; i < 5; i++) {
  bpf_map_lookup_and_delete(&stack_map, NULL, &value);
  printf("Value read from the map: '%d'\n", value);
}
```

This program prints the following:

```
Value read from the map: '4'
Value read from the map: '3'
Value read from the map: '2'
Value read from the map: '1'
Value read from the map: '0'
```

If we try to pop a new element from the map, `bpf_map_lookup_and_delete` will return a negative number, and the `errno` variable will be set to `ENOENT`.

These are all the map types that you can use in a BPF program. You'll find some of them more useful than others; it will depend on the kind of program that you're writing. We'll see more usage examples throughout the book that will help you cement the fundamentals that you just saw.

As we mentioned earlier, BPF maps are stored as regular files in your operating system. We have not talked about the specific characteristics of the filesystem that the kernel uses to save maps and programs. The next section guides you through the BPF filesystem, and the type of persistence that you can expect from it.

The BPF Virtual Filesystem

A fundamental characteristic of BPF maps is that being based on file descriptors means that when a descriptor is closed, the map and all the information it holds disappear. The original implementation of BPF maps was focused on short-lived isolated programs that didn't share any information among one another. Erasing all data when the file descriptor was closed made a lot of sense in those scenarios. However, with the introduction of more complex maps and integrations within the kernel, its developers realized that they needed a way to save the information that maps held, even after a program terminated and closed the map's file descriptor. Version 4.4 of the Linux kernel introduced two new syscalls to allow pinning and fetching maps and BPF programs from a virtual filesystem. Maps and BPF programs pinned to this filesystem will remain in memory after the program that created them terminates. In this section we explain how to work with this virtual filesystem.

The default directory where BPF expects to find this virtual filesystem is */sys/fs/bpf*. Some Linux distributions don't mount this filesystem by default because they don't assume that the kernel supports BPF. You can mount it yourself by using the mount command:

```
# mount -t bpf /sys/fs/bpf /sys/fs/bpf
```

Like any other file hierarchy, persistent BPF objects in the filesystem are identified by paths. You can organize these paths in any way that makes sense for your programs. For example, if you want to share a specific map with IP information between programs, you might want to store it in */sys/fs/bpf/shared/ips*. As we mentioned earlier, there are two types of objects that you can save in this filesystem: BPF maps and full BPF programs. Both of these are identified by file descriptors, so the interface to work with them is the same. These objects can be manipulated only by the bpf syscall. Although the kernel provides high-level helpers to assist you in interacting with them, you cannot do things like trying to open these files with the open syscall.

BPF_PIN_FD is the command to save BPF objects in this filesystem. When the command succeeds, the object will be visible in the filesystem in the path that you specified. If the command fails, it returns a negative number, and the global errno variable is set with the error code.

BPF_OBJ_GET is the command to fetch BPF objects that have been pinned to the filesystem. This command uses the path you assigned the object to to load it. When this command succeeds, it returns the file descriptor identifier associated to the object. If it fails, it returns a negative number, and the global errno variable is set with the specific error code.

Let's see an example of how to take advantage of these two commands in different programs using the helper functions that the kernel provides.

First, we're going to write a program that creates a map, populates it with several elements, and saves it in the filesystem:

```
static const char * file_path = "/sys/fs/bpf/my_array";

int main(int argc, char **argv) {
  int key, value, fd, added, pinned;

  fd = bpf_create_map(BPF_MAP_TYPE_ARRAY, sizeof(int), sizeof(int), 100, 0); ❶
  if (fd < 0) {
    printf("Failed to create map: %d (%s)\n", fd, strerror(errno));
    return -1;
  }

  key = 1, value = 1234;
  added = bpf_map_update_elem(fd, &key, &value, BPF_ANY);
  if (added < 0) {
    printf("Failed to update map: %d (%s)\n", added, strerror(errno));
    return -1;
  }
```

```
  pinned = bpf_obj_pin(fd, file_path);
  if (pinned < 0) {
    printf("Failed to pin map to the file system: %d (%s)\n",
        pinned, strerror(errno));
    return -1;
  }

  return 0;
}
```

❶ This section of code should already look familiar to you from our previous examples. First, we create a hash-table map with a fixed size of one element. Then we update the map to add only that element. If we tried to add more elements, bpf_map_update_elem would fail because we would be overflowing the map.

We use the helper function pbf_obj_pin to save the map in the filesystem. You can actually check that you have a new file under that path in your machine after the program has terminated:

```
ls -la /sys/fs/bpf
total 0
drwxrwxrwt 2 root  root  0 Nov 24 13:56 .
drwxr-xr-x 9 root  root  0 Nov 24 09:29 ..
-rw------- 1 david david 0 Nov 24 13:56 my_map
```

Now we can write a similar program that loads that map from the file system and prints the elements we inserted. That way we can verify that we saved the map correctly:

```
static const char * file_path = "/sys/fs/bpf/my_array";

int main(int argc, char **argv) {
  int fd, key, value, result;

  fd = bpf_obj_get(file_path);
  if (fd < 0) {
    printf("Failed to fetch the map: %d (%s)\n", fd, strerror(errno));
    return -1;
  }

  key = 1;
  result = bpf_map_lookup_elem(fd, &key, &value);
  if (result < 0) {
    printf("Failed to read value from the map: %d (%s)\n",
        result, strerror(errno));
    return -1;
  }

  printf("Value read from the map: '%d'\n", value);
  return 0;
```

Being able to save BPF objects in the filesystem opens the door to more interesting applications. Your data and programs are no longer tied to a single execution thread. Information can be shared by different applications, and BPF programs can run even after the application that created them terminates. This gives them an extra level or availability that would have not been possible without the BPF filesystem.

Conclusion

Establishing communication channels between the kernel and user-space is fundamental to take full advantage of any BPF program. In this chapter you learned how to create BPF maps to establish that communication and how to work with them. We've also described the types of maps that you can use in your programs. As you progress in the book, you'll see more specific map examples. Finally, you learned how to pin entire maps to the system to make them and the information they hold durable to crashes and interruptions.

BPF maps are the central bus of communication between the kernel and user-space. In this chapter, we established the fundamental concepts that you need to know to understand them. In the next chapter we make more extensive use of these data structures to share data. We also introduce you to additional tools that will make working with BPF maps more efficient.

In the next chapter you'll see how BPF programs and maps work together to give you tracing capabilities on your systems from the kernel point of view. We explore different ways to attach programs to different entry points in the kernel. Finally, we cover how to represent multiple data points in a way that makes your applications easier to debug and observe.

CHAPTER 4

Tracing with BPF

In software engineering, tracing is a method to collect data for profiling and debugging. The objective is to provide useful information at runtime for future analysis. The main advantage of using BPF for tracing is that you can access almost any piece of information from the Linux kernel and your applications. BPF adds a minimum amount of overhead to the system's performance and latency in comparison with other tracing technologies, and it doesn't require developers to modify their applications for the only purpose of gathering data from them.

The Linux kernel provides several instrumentation capabilities that can be used in conjunction with BPF. In this chapter we talk about these different capabilities. We show you how the kernel exposes those capabilities in your operating system so that you know how to find the information available to your BPF programs.

Tracing's end goal is to provide you with a deep understanding of any system by taking all of the available data and presenting it to you in a useful way. We're going to talk about a few different data representations and how you can use them in different scenarios.

Beginning in this chapter, we're going to use a powerful toolkit to write BPF programs, the BPF Compiler Collection (BCC). BCC is a set of components that makes building BPF programs more predictable. Even if you master Clang and LLVM, you won't probably want to spend more time than necessary building the same utilities and ensuring that the BPF verifier doesn't reject your programs. BCC provides reusable components for common structures, like Perf event maps, and integration with the LLVM backend to provide better debugging options. On top of that, BCC includes bindings for several programming languages; we're going to use Python in our examples. These bindings allow you to write the user-space part of your BPF programs in a high-level language, which results in more useful programs. We also use BCC in following chapters to make our examples more concise.

The first step to be able to trace programs in the Linux kernel is to identify the extension points that it provides for you to attach BPF programs. Those extension points are commonly called *probes*.

Probes

One of the definitions in the English dictionary for the word *probe* is as follows:

> An unmanned exploratory spacecraft designed to transmit information about its environment.

This definition evokes memories of sci-fi movies and epic NASA missions in our minds, and probably in yours too. When we talk about tracing probes, we can use a very similar definition.

> Tracing probes are exploratory programs designed to transmit information about the environment in which they are executed.

They collect data in your system and make it available for you to explore and analyze. Traditionally, using probes in Linux involved writing programs that were compiled into kernel modules, which could cause catastrophic problems in production systems. Over the years, they evolved to be safer to execute but still cumbersome to write and test. Tools like SystemTap established new protocols to write probes and paved the way to get much richer information from the Linux kernel and all programs running on user-space.

BPF piggybacks on tracing probes to collect information for debugging and analysis. The safety nature of BPF programs makes them more compelling to use than tools that still rely on recompiling the kernel. Re-compiling the kernel to include external modules can introduce a risk of crashes due to missbehaving code. The BPF verifier eliminates this risk by analyzing the program before loading in the kernel. The BPF developers took advantage of probe definitions, and modified the kernel to execute BPF programs rather than kernel modules when a code execution finds one of those definitions.

Understanding the different types of probes that you can define is fundamental to exploring what's happening within your system. In this section, we classify the different probe definitions, how to discover them in your system, and how to attach BPF programs to them.

In this chapter, we cover four different types of probes:

Kernel probes
    These give you dynamic access to internal components in the kernel.

Tracepoints
    These provide static access to internal components in the kernel.

User-space probes
   These give you dynamic access to programs running in user-space.

User statically defined tracepoints
   These allow static access to programs running in user-space.

Let's begin with kernel probes.

Kernel Probes

Kernel probes allow you to set dynamic flags, or breaks, in almost any kernel instruction with a minimum of overhead. When the kernel reaches one of these flags, it executes the code attached to the probe, and then resumes its usual routine. Kernel probes can give you information about anything happening in your system, such as files opened in your system and binaries being executed. One important thing to keep in mind about kernel probes is that they don't have a stable application binary interface (ABI), which means that they might change between kernel versions. The same code might stop working if you try to attach the same probe to two systems with two different kernel versions.

Kernel probes are divided into two categories: *kprobes* and *kretprobes*. Their use depends on where in the execution cycle you can insert your BPF program. This section guides you on how to use each one of them to attach BPF programs to those probes and extract information from the kernel.

Kprobes

Kprobes allow you to insert BPF programs before any kernel instruction is executed. You need to know the function signature that you want to break into, and as we mentioned earlier, this is not a stable ABI, so you'll want to be careful setting these probes if you're going to run the same program in different kernel versions. When the kernel execution arrives to the instruction where you set your probe, it sidesteps into your code, runs your BPF program, and returns the execution to the original instruction.

To show you how to use kprobes, we're going to write a BPF program that prints the name of any binary that's executed in your system. We're going to use the Python frontend for the BCC tools in this example, but you can write it with any other BPF tooling:

```
from bcc import BPF

bpf_source = """
int do_sys_execve(struct pt_regs *ctx, void filename, void argv, void envp) { ❶
  char comm[16];
  bpf_get_current_comm(&comm, sizeof(comm));
  bpf_trace_printk("executing program: %s", comm);
  return 0;
}
```

```
"""

bpf = BPF(text = bpf_source)        ❷
execve_function = bpf.get_syscall_fnname("execve")                    ❸
bpf.attach_kprobe(event = execve_function, fn_name = "do_sys_execve")   ❹
bpf.trace_print()
```

❶ Our BPF program starts. The helper `bpf_get_current_comm` is going to fetch the
   current command's name that the kernel is running and store it in our `comm` variable. We've defined this as a fixed-length array because the kernel has a 16-
   character limit for command names. After getting the command name, we print
   it in our debug trace, so the person running the Python script can see all commands captured by BPF.

❷ Load the BPF program into the kernel.

❸ Associate the program with the `execve` syscall. The name of this syscall has
   changed in different kernel versions, and BCC provides a function to retrieve this
   name without you having to remember which kernel version you're running.

❹ The code outputs the trace log, so you can see all of the commands that you're
   tracing with this program.

Kretprobes

Kretprobes are going to insert your BPF program when a kernel instruction returns a
value after being executed. Usually, you'll want to combine both kprobes and kretprobes into a single BPF program so that you have a full picture of the instruction's
behavior.

We're going to use a similar example to the one in the previous section to show you
how kretprobes work:

```
from bcc import BPF

bpf_source = """
int ret_sys_execve(struct pt_regs *ctx) {        ❶
  int return_value;
  char comm[16];
  bpf_get_current_comm(&comm, sizeof(comm));
  return_value = PT_REGS_RC(ctx);

  bpf_trace_printk("program: %s, return: %d", comm, return_value);
  return 0;
}
"""

bpf = BPF(text = bpf_source)        ❷
```

```
execve_function = bpf.get_syscall_fnname("execve")
bpf.attach_kretprobe(event = execve_function, fn_name = "ret_sys_execve")  ❸
bpf.trace_print()
```

❶ Define the function that implements the BPF program. The kernel will execute it
    immediately after the execve syscall finishes. PT_REGS_RC is a macro that's going
    to read the returned value from BPF register for this specific context. We also use
    bpf_trace_printk to print the command and its returned value in our debug
    log.

❷ Initialize the BPF program and load it in the kernel.

❸ Change the attachment function to attach_kretprobe.

What's That Context Argument?

You might have noticed that both BPF programs have the same first argument in the
attached function, identified as ctx. This parameter (called context) is going to give
you access to the information that the kernel is currently processing. Therefore, this
context is going to depend on the type of BPF program you're running at the time.
The CPU will store different information about the current task that the kernel is executing. This structure also depends on your system architecture; an ARM processor
will include a different set of registers than an x64 processor. You can access those
registers without having to worry about the architecture with macros defined by the
kernel, like PT_REGS_RC.

Kernel probes are a powerful way to access the kernel. But as we mentioned earlier,
they might be unstable because you're attaching to dynamic points in the kernel's
source that might change or disappear from one version to another. Now you'll see a
different method to attach programs to the kernel that is safer.

Tracepoints

Tracepoints are static markers in the kernel's code that you can use to attach code in a
running kernel. The main difference with kprobes is that they are codified by the kernel developers when they implement changes in the kernel; that's why we refer to
them as static. Because they are static, the ABI for tracepoints is more stable; the kernel always guarantees that a tracepoint in an old version is going to exist in new versions. However, given that developers need to add them to the kernel, they might not
cover all the subsystems that form the kernel.

As we mentioned in Chapter 2, you can see all of the available tracepoints in your
system by listing all the files in */sys/kernel/debug/tracing/events*. For example, you can

find all of the tracepoints for BPF itself by listing the events defined in */sys/kernel/debug/tracing/events/bpf*:

```
sudo ls -la /sys/kernel/debug/tracing/events/bpf
total 0
drwxr-xr-x  14 root root 0 Feb  4 16:13 .
drwxr-xr-x 106 root root 0 Feb  4 16:14 ..
drwxr-xr-x   2 root root 0 Feb  4 16:13 bpf_map_create
drwxr-xr-x   2 root root 0 Feb  4 16:13 bpf_map_delete_elem
drwxr-xr-x   2 root root 0 Feb  4 16:13 bpf_map_lookup_elem
drwxr-xr-x   2 root root 0 Feb  4 16:13 bpf_map_next_key
drwxr-xr-x   2 root root 0 Feb  4 16:13 bpf_map_update_elem
drwxr-xr-x   2 root root 0 Feb  4 16:13 bpf_obj_get_map
drwxr-xr-x   2 root root 0 Feb  4 16:13 bpf_obj_get_prog
drwxr-xr-x   2 root root 0 Feb  4 16:13 bpf_obj_pin_map
drwxr-xr-x   2 root root 0 Feb  4 16:13 bpf_obj_pin_prog
drwxr-xr-x   2 root root 0 Feb  4 16:13 bpf_prog_get_type
drwxr-xr-x   2 root root 0 Feb  4 16:13 bpf_prog_load
drwxr-xr-x   2 root root 0 Feb  4 16:13 bpf_prog_put_rcu
-rw-r--r--   1 root root 0 Feb  4 16:13 enable
-rw-r--r--   1 root root 0 Feb  4 16:13 filter
```

Every subdirectory listed in that output corresponds to a tracepoint that we can attach BPF programs to. But there are two additional files there. The first file, `enable`, allows you to enable and disable all tracepoints for the BPF subsystem. If the content of the file is 0, the tracepoints are disabled; if the content of the file is 1, the tracepoints are enabled. The *filter* file allows you to write expressions that the Trace subsystem in the kernel will use to filter events. BPF doesn't use this file; read more in the kernel's tracing documentation (*https://oreil.ly/miNRd*).

Writing BPF programs to take advantage of tracepoints is similar to tracing with kprobes. Here's an example that uses a BPF program to trace all of the applications in your system that load other BPF programs:

```
from bcc import BPF

bpf_source = """
int trace_bpf_prog_load(void ctx) {        ❶
  char comm[16];
  bpf_get_current_comm(&comm, sizeof(comm));

  bpf_trace_printk("%s is loading a BPF program", comm);
  return 0;
}
"""

bpf = BPF(text = bpf_source)
bpf.attach_tracepoint(tp = "bpf:bpf_prog_load",
                      fn_name = "trace_bpf_prog_load")  ❷
bpf.trace_print()
```

❶ Declare the function that defines the BPF program. This code must look familiar to you already; there are only a few syntactic changes from the first example you saw when we talked about kprobes.

❷ The main difference in this program: instead of attaching the program to a kprobe, we're attaching it to a tracepoint. BCC follows a convention to name tracepoints; first you specify the subsystem to trace—bpf in this case—followed by a colon, followed by the tracepoint in the subsystem, `pbf_prog_load`. This means that every time the kernel executes the function `bpf_prog_load`, this program will receive the event, and it will print the name of the application that's executing that `bpf_prog_load` instruction.

Kernel probes and tracepoints are going to give you full access to the kernel. We recommend that you to use tracepoints whenever possible, but don't feel obligated to stick to tracepoints only because they are safer. Take advantage of the dynamic nature of the kernel probes. In the next section we discuss how to get a similar level of visibility in programs running in user-space.

User-Space Probes

User-space probes allow you to set dynamic flags in programs running in user-space. They are the equivalent of kernel-probes for instrumenting programs that run outside the kernel. When you define a uprobe, the kernel creates a trap around the attached instruction. When your application reaches that instruction, the kernel triggers an event that has your probe function as a callback. Uprobes also give you access to any library that your program is linked to, and you can trace those calls if you know the correct name for the instruction.

Much like kernel probes, user-space probes are also divided in two categories, uprobes and uretprobes, depending on where in the execution cycle you can insert your BPF program. Let's jump right in with some examples.

Uprobes

Generally speaking, uprobes are hooks that the kernel inserts into a program's instruction set before a specific instruction is executed. You need to be careful when you attach uprobes to different versions of the same program because function signatures might change internally between those versions. The only way to guarantee that a BPF program is going to run in two different versions is to ensure that the signature has not changed. You can use the command nm in Linux to list all the symbols included in an ELF object file, which is a good way to check whether the instruction that you're tracing still exists in your program, for example:

```
package main
import "fmt"
```

```
func main() {
        fmt.Println("Hello, BPF")
}
```

You can compile this Go program by using `go build -o hello-bpf main.go`. You can use the command `nm` to get information about all the instruction points that the binary file includes. `nm` is a program included in the GNU Development Tools that lists symbols from object files. If you filter the symbols with `main` in their name, you get a list similar to this one:

```
nm hello-bpf | grep main
0000000004850b0 T main.init
00000000567f06 B main.initdone.
00000000485040 T main.main
000000004c84a0 R main.statictmp_0
00000000428660 T runtime.main
0000000044da30 T runtime.main.func1
0000000044da80 T runtime.main.func2
000000000054b928 B runtime.main_init_done
00000000004c8180 R runtime.mainPC
0000000000567f1a B runtime.mainStarted
```

Now that you have a list of symbols, you can trace when they are executed, even between different processes executing the same binary.

To trace when the main function in our previous Go example is executed, we're going to write a BPF program, and we're going to attach it to a uprobe that will break before any process invokes that instruction:

```
from bcc import BPF

bpf_source = """
int trace_go_main(struct pt_regs *ctx) {
  u64 pid = bpf_get_current_pid_tgid();              ❶
  bpf_trace_printk("New hello-bpf process running with PID: %d", pid);
}
"""

bpf = BPF(text = bpf_source)
bpf.attach_uprobe(name = "hello-bpf",
    sym = "main.main", fn_name = "trace_go_main")      ❷
bpf.trace_print()
```

❶ Use the function `bpf_get_current_pid_tgid` to get the process identifier (PID) for the process that's running our `hello-bpf` program.

❷ Attach this program to a uprobe. This call needs to know that the object we want to trace, `hello-bpf`, is the absolute path to the object file. It also needs the symbol that we're tracing inside the object, `main.main` in this case, and the BPF program

---

that we want to run. With this, every time someone runs `hello-bpf` in our system, we'll get a new log in our trace pipe.

Uretprobes

Uretprobes are the parallel probe to kretprobes, but for user-space programs. They attach BPF programs to instructions that return values, and give you access to those returned values by accessing the registers from your BPF code.

Combining uprobes and uretprobes allows you to write more complex BPF programs. They can give you a more holistic view of applications running in your system. When you can inject tracing code before a function runs and immediately after it completes, you can begin gathering more data and measure application behaviors. A common use case is to measure how long a function takes to execute, without having to change a single line of code in your application.

We're going to reuse the Go program we wrote in "Uprobes" on page 53 to measure how long it takes to execute the main function. This BPF example is longer than the previous examples that you've seen, so we've divided it into different blocks of code:

```
bpf_source = """
int trace_go_main(struct pt_regs *ctx) {
  u64 pid = bpf_get_current_pid_tgid();
  bpf_trace_printk("New hello-bpf process running with PID: %d", pid); ❶
}
"""

bpf = BPF(text = bpf_source)
bpf.attach_uprobe(name = "hello-bpf",        ❷
    sym = "main.main", fn_name = "trace_go_main")      ❸
bpf.trace_print()
```

❶ Create a BPF hash map. This table allows us to share data between the uprobe and uretprobe functions. In this case we use the application PID as the table key, and we store the function start time as the value. The two most interesting operations in our uprobe function happen as described next.

❷ Capture the current time in the system in nanoseconds, as seen by the kernel.

❸ Create an entry in our cache with the program PID and the current time. We can assume that this time is the application's function start time. Let's declare our uretprobe function now:

Implement the function to attach when your instruction finishes. This uretprobe function is similar to others that you saw in "Kretprobes" on page 50:

```
bpf_source += """
static int print_duration(struct pt_regs *ctx) {
```

```
  u64 pid = bpf_get_current_pid_tgid();        ❶
  u64 start_time_ns = cache.lookup(&pid);
  if (start_time_ns == 0) {
    return 0;
  }
  u64 duration_ns = bpf_ktime_get_ns() - start_time_ns;
  bpf_trace_printk("Function call duration: %d", duration_ns);    ❷
  return 0;        ❸
}
"""
```

❶ Obtain the PID for our application; we need it to find its starting time. We use the map function lookup to fetch that time from the map where we stored it before the function ran.

❷ Calculate the function duration by subtracting that time from the current time.

❸ Print the latency in our trace log so we can display it in the terminal.

Now, the rest of the program needs to attach these two BPF functions to the right probes:

```
bpf = BPF(text = bpf_source)
bpf.attach_uprobe(name = "hello-bpf", sym = "main.main",
          fn_name = "trace_start_time")
bpf.attach_uretprobe(name = "hello-bpf", sym = "main.main",
          fn_name = "print_duration")
bpf.trace_print()
```

We've added a line to our original uprobe example where we're attaching our print function to the uretprobe for our application.

In this section you saw how to trace operations that happen in user-space with BPF. By combining BPF functions that are executed at different points in your application's lifecycle, you can begin extracting much richer information from it. However, as we mentioned at the beginning of this section, user-space probes are powerful, but they are also unstable. Our BPF examples can stop working only because someone decides to rename an application's function. Now let's look at a more stable way to trace user-space programs.

User Statically Defined Tracepoints

User statically defined tracepoints (USDTs) provide static tracepoints for applications in user-space. This is a convenient way to instrument applications because they give you a low-overhead entry point to the tracing capabilities that BPF offers. You can also use them as a convention to trace applications in production, regardless of the programming language with which these applications are written.

USDTs were popularized by DTrace, a tool originally developed at Sun Microsystems for dynamic instrumentation of Unix systems. DTrace was not available in Linux until recently due to licensing issues; however, the Linux kernel developers took a lot of inspiration from the original work in DTrace to implement USDTs.

Much like the static kernel tracepoints you saw earlier, USDTs require developers to instrument their code with instructions that the kernel will use as traps to execute BPF programs. The Hello World version of USDTs is only a few lines of code:

```
#include <sys/sdt.h>
int main() {
  DTRACE_PROBE("hello-usdt", "probe-main");
}
```

In this example, we're using a macro that Linux provides to define our first USDT. You can already see where the kernel takes inspiration from. DTRACE_PROBE is going to register the tracepoint that the kernel will use to inject our BPF function callback. The first argument in this macro is the program that's reporting the trace. The second one is the name of the trace that we're reporting.

Many applications that you might have installed in your system use this type of probe to give you access to runtime tracing data in a predictable way. The popular database MySQL, for example, exposes all kinds of information using statically defined tracepoints. You can gather information from queries executed in the server as well as from many other user operations. Node.js, the JavaScript runtime built on top of Chrome's V8 engine, also provides tracepoints that you can use to extract runtime information.

Before showing you how to attach BPF programs to user-defined tracepoint, we need to talk about discoverability. Because these tracepoints are defined in binary format inside the executable files, we need a way to list the probes defined by a program without having to dig through the source code. One way to extract this information is by reading the ELF binary directly. First, we're going to compile our previous Hello World USDT example; we can use GCC for that:

```
gcc -o hello_usdt hello_usdt.c
```

This command is going to generate a binary file called *hello_usdt* that we can use to start playing with several tools to discover the tracepoints that it defines. Linux provides a utility called readelf to show you information about ELF files. You can use it with our compiled example:

```
readelf -n ./hello_usdt
```

You can see the USDT that we defined in the output of this command:

```
Displaying notes found in: .note.stapsdt
  Owner                 Data size          Description
  stapsdt               0x00000033         NT_STAPSDT (SystemTap probe descriptors)
```

```
Provider: "hello-usdt"
Name: "probe-main"
```

readelf can give you a lot of information about a binary file; in our small example, it shows only a few lines of information, but its output becomes cumbersome to parse for more complicated binaries.

A better option to discover the tracepoints defined in a binary file is to use BCC's tplist tool, which can display both kernel tracepoints and USDTs. The advantage of this tool is the simplicity of its output; it shows you only tracepoint definitions, without any additional information about the executable. Its usage is similar to readelf:

```
tplist -l ./hello_usdt
```

It lists every tracepoint that you define in individual lines. In our example, it displays only a single line with our probe-main definition:

```
./hello_usdt "hello-usdt":"probe-main"
```

After you know the supported tracepoints in your binary, you can attach BPF programs to them in a similar way to what you've seen in previous examples:

```
from bcc import BPF, USDT

bpf_source = """
#include <uapi/linux/ptrace.h>
int trace_binary_exec(struct pt_regs *ctx) {
  u64 pid = bpf_get_current_pid_tgid();
  bpf_trace_printk("New hello_usdt process running with PID: %d", pid);
}
"""

usdt = USDT(path = "./hello_usdt")                                          ❶
usdt.enable_probe(probe = "probe-main", fn_name = "trace_binary_exec")      ❷
bpf = BPF(text = bpf_source, usdt = usdt)                                   ❸
bpf.trace_print()
```

There is a major change in this example that requires some explanation.

❶ Create a USDT object; we haven't done this in our previous examples. USDTs are not part of BPF, in the sense that you can use them without having to interact with the BPF VM. Because they are independent of one another, it makes sense that their usage is independent of the BPF code.

❷ Attach the BPF function to trace program executions to the probe in our application.

❸ Initialize our BPF environment with the tracepoint definition that we just created. This will inform BCC that it needs to generate the code to connect our BPF

---

program with the probe definition in our binary file. When both of them are connected, we can print the traces generated by our BPF program to discover new executions of our binary example.

USDTs bindings for other languages

You can also use USDTs to trace applications written with programming languages besides C. You'll be able to find bindings for Python, Ruby, Go, Node.js, and many other languages in GitHub. The Ruby bindings are one of our favorites because of their simplicity and interoperability with frameworks such as Rails. Dale Hamel, who currently works at Shopify, wrote an excellent report about the usage of USDTs in his blog (*https://oreil.ly/7pgNO*). He also maintains a library called *ruby-static-tracing* (*https://oreil.ly/ge6cu*) that makes tracing Ruby and Rails applications even more straightforward.

Hamel's static tracing library allows you to inject tracing capabilities at the class level without requiring you to add the tracing logic to every method in that class. In complex scenarios, it also gives you convenient methods to register dedicated tracing endpoints yourself.

To use `ruby-static-tracing` in your applications, first you need to configure when the tracepoints are going to be enabled. You can turn them on by default when the application starts, but if you want to avoid the overhead of collecting data all the time, you can activate them using a syscall signal. Hamel recommends using PROF as this signal:

```
require 'ruby-static-tracing'

StaticTracing.configure do |config|
  config.mode = StaticTracing::Configuration::Modes::SIGNAL
  config.signal = StaticTracing::Configuration::Modes::SIGNALS::SIGPROF
end
```

With this configuration in place, you can use the `kill` command to enable your application's static tracepoints on demand. In the next example, we assume that there is only a Ruby process running on our machine, and we can get its process identifier using `pgrep`:

```
kill -SIGPROF `pgrep -nx ruby`
```

Besides configuring when the tracepoints are active, you might want to use some of the built-in tracing mechanisms that *ruby-static-tracing* provides. At the time of writing this, the library incorporates tracepoints to measure latency and to collect stack traces. We really like how a tedious task such as measuring function latency becomes almost trivial by using this built-in module. First, you need to add the latency tracer to your initial configuration:

```
require 'ruby-static-tracing'
require 'ruby-static-tracing/tracer/concerns/latency_tracer'

StaticTracing.configure do |config|
  config.add_tracer(StaticTracing::Tracer::Latency)
end
```

After that, every class that includes the latency module generates static tracepoints for each public method defined. When tracing is enabled, you can query those tracepoints to collect timing data. In our next example, `ruby-static-tracing` generates a static tracepoint named `usdt:/proc/X/fd/Y:user_model:find`, following the convention of using the class name as the namespace for the tracepoint and using the method name as the tracepoint name:

```
class UserModel
  def find(id)
  end

  include StaticTracing::Tracer::Concerns::Latency
end
```

Now we can use BCC to extract the latency information for each call to our `find` method. To do that, we use BCC's built-in functions `bpf_usdt_readarg` and `bpf_usdt_readarg_p`. These functions read the arguments set each time our application's code is executed. `ruby-static-tracing` always sets the method name as the first argument for the tracepoint, whereas it sets the calculated value as the second argument. The next snippet implements the BPF program that gets the tracepoint information and prints it in the tracing log:

```
bpf_source = """
#include <uapi/linux/ptrace.h>
int trace_latency(struct pt_regs *ctx) {
  char method[64];
  u64 latency;

  bpf_usdt_readarg_p(1, ctx, &method, sizeof(method));
  bpf_usdt_readarg(2, ctx, &latency);

  bpf_trace_printk("method %s took %d ms", method, latency);
}
"""
```

We also need to load the previous BPF program into the kernel. Because we're tracing a specific application that's already running in our machine, we can attach the program to the specific process identifier:

```
parser = argparse.ArgumentParser()
parser.add_argument("-p", "--pid", type = int, help = "Process ID")      ❶
args = parser.parse_args()

usdt = USDT(pid = int(args.pid))
```

```
usdt.enable_probe(probe = "latency", fn_name = "trace_latency")    ❷
bpf = BPF(text = bpf_source, usdt = usdt)
bpf.trace_print()
```

❶ Specify that PID.

❷ Enable the probe, load the program into the kernel, and print the tracing log.
    (This section is very similar to the one you saw earlier.)

In this section, we've shown you how to introspect applications that define tracepoints statically. Many well-known libraries and programing languages include these
probes to help you debug running applications, gaining more visibility when they run
in production environments. This is only the tip of the iceberg; after you have the
data, you need to make sense of it. This is what we explore next.

Visualizing Tracing Data

So far, we've shown examples that print data in our debug output. This is not very
useful in production environments. You want to make sense of that data, but nobody
likes to make sense of long and complicated logs. If we want to monitor changes in
latency and CPU utilization, it's easier to do it by looking at graphs over a time period
than aggregating numbers from a file stream.

This section explores different ways to present BPF tracing data. On one hand, we'll
show you how BPF programs can structure information in aggregates for you. On the
other hand, you'll learn how to export that information in a portable representation
and use off-the-shelf tools to access a richer representation and share your findings
with other people.

Flame Graphs

Flame graphs are diagrams that help you visualize how your system is spending time.
They can give you a clear representation of which code in an application is executed
more often. Brendan Gregg, the creator of flame graphs, maintains a set of scripts to
easily generate these visualization formats on GitHub (*https://oreil.ly/3iiZx*). We use
those scripts to generate flame graphs from data collected with BPF later in this section. You can see what these graphs look like in Figure 4-1.

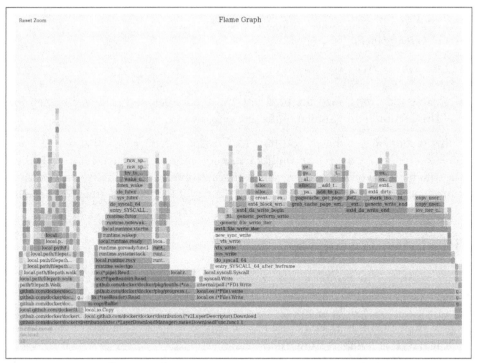

Figure 4-1. A CPU flame graph

There are two important things to remember about what a flame graph shows:

- The x-axis is ordered alphabetically. The width of each stack represents how often it appears in the collect data, which can be correlated to how often that code path has been visited while the profiler was enabled.

- The y-axis shows the stack traces ordered as the profiler reads them, preserving the trace hierarchy.

The most well-known flame graphs represent the most frequent code consuming CPU in your system; these are called *on-CPU graphs*. Another interesting flame graph visualization is *off-CPU graphs*; they represent the time that a CPU spends on other tasks that are not related to your application. By combining on-CPU and off-CPU graphs, you can get a complete view of what your system is spending CPU cycles on.

Both, on-CPU and off-CPU graphs use stack traces to indicate where the system is spending time. Some programming languages, such as Go, always include trace information in their binaries, but others, such as C++ and Java, require some extra work to make stack traces readable. After your application includes stack trace information, BPF programs can use it to aggregate the most frequent code paths as seen by the kernel.

There are advantages and disadvantages to stack trace aggregation in the kernel. On one hand, it's an efficient way to count stack trace frequency because it happens in the kernel, avoiding sending every stack information to user-space and reducing the data interchange between the kernel and user-space. On the other hand, the number of events to process for off-CPU graphs can be significantly high, because you're keeping track of every event that occurs during your application's context switch. This can create significant overhead in your system if you try to profile it for too long. Keep this in mind when you're working with flame graphs.

BCC provides several utilities to help you aggregate and visualize stack traces, but the main one is the macro `BPF_STACK_TRACE`. This macro generates a BPF map of type `BPF_MAP_TYPE_STACK_TRACE` to store the stacks that your BPF program accumulates. On top of that, this BPF map is enhanced with methods to extract the stack information from the program's context and walk the stack traces accumulated when you want to use them after aggregating them.

In the next example, we build a simple BPF profiler that prints the stack traces collected from user-space applications. We generate on-CPU flame graphs with the traces that our profiler collects. To test this profiler, we're going to write a minimal Go program that generates CPU load. This is the code for that minimal application:

```
package main

import "time"

func main() {
        j := 3
        for time.Since(time.Now()) < time.Second {
                for i := 1; i < 1000000; i++ {
                        j *= i
                }
        }
}
```

If you save this code in a file called *main.go* and run it with `go run main.go`, you'll see that your system's CPU utilization increases significantly. You can stop the execution by pressing Ctrl-C on your keyboard, and the CPU utilization will go back to normal.

The first part of our BPF program is going to initialize the profiler structures:

```
bpf_source = """
#include <uapi/linux/ptrace.h>
#include <uapi/linux/bpf_perf_event.h>
#include <linux/sched.h>

struct trace_t { ❶
```

```
    int stack_id;
}

BPF_HASH(cache, struct trace_t);        ❷
BPF_STACK_TRACE(traces, 10000);         ❸
"""
```

❶ Initialize a structure that will store the reference identifier for each one of the
stack frames that our profiler receives. We use these identifiers later to find out
which code path was being executed at that time.

❷ Initialize a BPF hash map that we use to aggregate how often we see the same
strack frame. The flame graph scripts use this aggregated value to determine how
frequent the same code is executed.

❸ Initialize our BPF stack trace map. We're setting a maximum size for this map,
but it can vary depending on how much data you want to process. It would be
better to have this value as a variable, but we know that our Go application is not
very big, so 10,000 elements is plenty.

Next, we implement the function that aggregates stack traces in our profiler:

```
bpf_source += """
int collect_stack_traces(struct bpf_perf_event_data *ctx) {
  u32 pid = bpf_get_current_pid_tgid() >> 32;        ❶
  if (pid != PROGRAM_PID)
    return 0;

  struct trace_t trace = {        ❷
    .stack_id = traces.get_stackid(&ctx->regs, BPF_F_USER_STACK)
  };

  cache.increment(trace);        ❸
  return 0;
}
"""
```

❶ Verify that the process ID for the program in the current BPF context is the one
for our Go application; otherwise, we ignore the event. We have not defined the
value for PROGRAM_PID at the moment. Let's replace this string in the Python part
of the profiler before initializing the BPF program. This is a current limitation in
the way BCC initializes BPF program; we cannot pass any variables from user-
space, and as a common practice, these strings are replaced in the code before
initialization.

❷ Create a trace to aggregate its usage. We fetch the stack ID from the program's
context with the built-in function get_stackid. This is one of the helpers that
BCC adds to our stack trace map. We use the flag BPF_F_USER_STACK to indicate

that we want to get the stack ID for the user-space application, and we don't care about what happens inside the kernel.

❸ Increment the counter for our trace to keep track of how often the same code is being exercised.

Next, we're going to attach our stack trace collector to all Perf events in the kernel:

```
program_pid = int(sys.argv[0])               ❶
bpf_source = bpf_source.replace('PROGRAM_PID', program_pid) ❷

bpf = BPF(text = bpf_source)
bpf.attach_perf_event(ev_type = PerfType.SOFTWARE,   ❸
                      ev_config = PerfSWConfig.CPU_CLOCK,
                      fn_name = 'collect_stack_traces')
```

❶ The first argument for our Python program. This is the process identifier for the Go application that we're profiling.

❷ Use Python's built-in `replace` function to swap the string PROGRAM_ID in our BPF source with the argument provided to the profiler.

❸ Attach the BPF program to all Software Perf events, this will ignore any other events, like Hardware events. We're also configuring our BPF program to use the CPU clock as time source so we can measure execution time.

Finally, we need to implement the code that will dump the stack traces in our standard output when the profiler is interrupted:

```
try:
  sleep(99999999)
except KeyboardInterrupt:
  signal.signal(signal.SIGINT, signal_ignore)

for trace, acc in sorted(cache.items(), key=lambda cache: cache[1].value): ❶
  line = []                                                              
  if trace.stack_id < 0 and trace.stack_id == -errno.EFAULT             ❷
    line = ['Unknown stack']
  else
    stack_trace = list(traces.walk(trace.stack_id))
    for stack_address in reversed(stack_trace)                          ❸
      line.extend(bpf.sym(stack_address, program_pid))                  ❹

  frame = b";".join(line).decode('utf-8', 'replace')                    ❺
  print("%s %d" % (frame, acc.value))
```

❶ Iterate over all the traces we collected so that we can print them in order.

❷ Validate that we got stack identifiers that we can correlate with specific lines of code later. If we get an invalid value, we'll use a placeholder in our flame graph.

❸ Iterate over all the entries in the stack trace in reverse order. We do this because we want to see the first most recently executed code path at the top, like you'd expect in any stack trace.

❹ Use the BCC helper `sym` to translate the memory address for the stack frame into a function name in our source code.

❺ Format the stack trace line separated by semicolons. This is the format that the flame graph scripts expect later to be able to generate our visualization.

With our BPF profiler complete, we can run it as `sudo` to collect stack traces for our busy Go program. We need to pass the Go program's process ID to our profiler to make sure that we collect only traces for this application; we can find that PID using `pgrep`. This is how you run the profiler if you save it in a file called *profiler.py*:

```
./profiler.py `pgrep -nx go` > /tmp/profile.out
```

`pgrep` will search the PID for a process running on your system whose name matches `go`. We send our profiler's output to a temporary file so that we can generate the flame graph visualization.

As we mentioned earlier, we're going to use Brendan Gregg's FlameGraph scripts to generate an SVG file for our graph; you can find those scripts in his GitHub repository (*https://oreil.ly/orqcb*). After you've downloaded that repository, you can use `flamegraph.pl` to generate the graph. You can open the graph with your favorite browser; we're using Firefox in this example:

```
./flamegraph.pl /tmp/profile.out > /tmp/flamegraph.svg && \
    firefox /tmp/flamefraph.svg
```

This kind of profiler is useful for tracing performance issues in your system. BCC already includes a more advanced profiler than the one in our example that you can use in your production environments directly. Besides the profiler, BCC includes tools to help you generate off-CPU flame graphs and many other visualizations to analyze systems.

Flame graphs are useful for performance analysis. We use them frequently in our day-to-day work. In many scenarios, besides visualizing hot code paths, you'll want to measure how often events in your systems occur. We focus on that next.

Histograms

Histograms are diagrams that show you how frequently several ranges of values occur. The numeric data to represent this is divided into buckets, and each bucket contains the number of occurrences of any data point within the bucket. The frequency that histograms measure is the combination of the height and width of each bucket. If the buckets are divided in equal ranges, this frequency matches the histogram's height, but if the ranges are not divided equally, you need to multiply each height by each width to find the correct frequency.

Histograms are a fundamental component to do systems performance analysis. They are a great tool to represent the distribution of measurable events, like instruction latency, because they show you more correct information than you can get with other measurements, like averages.

BPF programs can create histograms based on many metrics. You can use BPF maps to collect the information, classify it in buckets, and then generate the histogram representation for your data. Implementing this logic is not complicated, but it becomes tedious if you want to print histograms every time you need to analyze a program's output. BCC includes an implementation out of the box that you can reuse in every program, without having to calculate bucketing and frequency manually every single time. However, the kernel source has a fantastic implementation that we encourage you to check out in the BPF samples.

As a fun experiment, we're going to show you how to use BCC's histograms to visualize the latency introduced by loading BPF programs when an application calls the `bpf_prog_load` instruction. We use kprobes to collect how long it takes for that instruction to complete, and we'll accumulate the results in a histogram that we'll visualize later. We've divided this example into several parts to make it easier to follow.

This first part includes the initial source for our BPF program:

```
bpf_source = """
#include <uapi/linux/ptrace.h>

BPF_HASH(cache, u64, u64);
BPF_HISTOGRAM(histogram);

int trace_bpf_prog_load_start(void ctx) {          ❶
  u64 pid = bpf_get_current_pid_tgid();            ❷
  u64 start_time_ns = bpf_ktime_get_ns();
  cache.update(&pid, &start_time_ns);              ❸
  return 0;
}
"""
```

❶ Use a macro to create a BPF hash map to store the initial time when the `bpf_prog_load` instruction is triggered.

❷ Use a new macro to create a BPF histogram map. This is not a native BPF map; BCC includes this macro to make it easier for you to create these visualizations. Under the hood, this BPF histogram uses array maps to store the information. It also has several helpers to do the bucketing and create the final graph.

❸ Use the programs PID to store when the application triggers the instruction we want to trace. (This function will look familiar to you—we took it from the previous Uprobes example.),

Let's see how we calculate the delta for the latency and store it in our histogram. The initial lines of this new block of code will also look familiar because we're still following the example we talked about in "Uprobes" on page 53.

```
bpf_source += """
int trace_bpf_prog_load_return(void ctx) {
  u64 *start_time_ns, delta;
  u64 pid = bpf_get_current_pid_tgid();
  start_time_ns = cache.lookup(&pid);
  if (start_time_ns == 0)
    return 0;

  delta = bpf_ktime_get_ns() - *start_time_ns;        ❶
  histogram.increment(bpf_log2l(delta));              ❷
  return 0;
}
"""
```

❶ Calculate the delta between the time the instruction was invoked and the time it took our program to arrive here; we can assume that it's also the time the instruction completed.

❷ Store that delta in our histogram. We do two operations in this line. First, we use the built-in function `bpf_log2l` to generate the bucket identifier for the value of the delta. This function creates a stable distribution of values over time. Then, we use the `increment` function to add a new item to this bucket. By default, `increment` adds 1 to the value if the bucket existed in the histogram, or it starts a new bucket with the value of 1, so you don't need to worry about whether the value exists in advance.

The last piece of code that we need to write attaches these two functions to the valid kprobes and prints the histogram on the screen so that we can see the latency distribution. This section is where we initialize our BPF program and we wait for events to generate the histogram:

```
bpf = BPF(text = bpf_source)                        ❶
bpf.attach_kprobe(event = "bpf_prog_load",
    fn_name = "trace_bpf_prog_load_start")
bpf.attach_kretprobe(event = "bpf_prog_load",
    fn_name = "trace_bpf_prog_load_return")

try:                                                ❷
  sleep(99999999)
except KeyboardInterrupt:
  print()

bpf["histogram"].print_log2_hist("msecs")           ❸
```

❶ Initialize BPF and attach our functions to kprobes.

❷ Make our program wait so that we can gather as many events as we need from our system.

❸ Print the histogram map in our terminal with the traced distribution of events—this is another BCC macro that allows us to get the histogram map.

As we mentioned at the beginning of this section, histograms can be useful to observe anomalies in your system. The BCC tools include numerous scripts that make use of histograms to represent data; we highly recommend you take a look at them when you need inspiration to dive into your system.

Perf Events

We believe that Perf events are probably the most important communication method that you need to master to use BPF tracing successfully. We talked about BPF Perf event array maps in the previous chapter. They allow you to put data in a buffer ring that's synchronized in real time with user-space programs. This is ideal when you're collecting a large amount of data in your BPF program and want to offload processing and visualization to a user-space program. That will allow you to have more control over the presentation layer because you're not restricted by the BPF VM regarding programming capabilities. Most of the BPF tracing programs that you can find use Perf events only for this purpose.

Here, we show you how to use them to extract information about binary execution and classify that information to print which binaries are the most executed in your system. We've divided this example into two blocks of code so that you can easily follow the example. In the first block, we define our BPF program and attach it to a kprobe, like we did in "Probes" on page 48:

```
bpf_source = """
#include <uapi/linux/ptrace.h>

BPF_PERF_OUTPUT(events);                             ❶
```

```
int do_sys_execve(struct pt_regs *ctx, void filename, void argv, void envp) {
  char comm[16];
  bpf_get_current_comm(&comm, sizeof(comm));

  events.perf_submit(ctx, &comm, sizeof(comm));              ❷
  return 0;
}
"""

bpf = BPF(text = bpf_source)                                 ❸
execve_function = bpf.get_syscall_fnname("execve")
bpf.attach_kprobe(event = execve_function, fn_name = "do_sys_execve")
```

In the first line of this example, we're importing a library from Python's standard library. We're going to use a Python counter to aggregate the events we're receiving from our BPF program.

❶ Use `BPF_PERF_OUTPUT` to declare a Perf events map. This is a convinient macro that BCC provides to declare this kind of map. We're naming this map *events*.

❷ Send it to user-space for aggregation after we have the name of the program that the kernel has executed. We do that with `perf_submit`. This function updates the Perf events map with our new piece of information.

❸ Initialize the BPF program and attach it to the kprobe to be triggered when a new program is executed in our system.

Now that we have written the code to collect all programs that are executed in our system, we need to aggregate them in user-space. There is a lot of information in the next code snippet, so we're going to walk you through the most important lines:

```
from collections import Counter
aggregates = Counter()                                       ❶

def aggregate_programs(cpu, data, size):                     ❷
  comm = bpf["events"].event(data)                           ❸
  aggregates[comm] += 1

bpf["events"].open_perf_buffer(aggregate_programs)           ❹
while True:
    try:
      bpf.perf_buffer_poll()
    except KeyboardInterrupt:                                ❺
      break

for (comm, times) in aggregates.most_common():
  print("Program {} executed {} times".format(comm, times))
```

❶ Declare a counter to store our program information. We use the name of the program as the key, and the values will be counters. We use the `aggregate_programs` function to collect the data from the Perf events map. In this example, you can see how we use the BCC macro to access the map and extract the next incoming data event from the top of the stack.

❷ Increment the number of times we've received an event with the same program name.

❸ Use the function `open_perf_buffer` to tell BCC that it needs to execute the function `aggregate_programs` every time it receives an event from the Perf events map.

❹ BCC polls events after opening the ring buffer until we interrupt this Python program. The longer you wait, the more information you're going to process. You can see how we use `perf_buffer_poll` for this purpose.

❺ Use the `most_common` function to get the list of elements in the counter and loop to print the top executed programs in your system first.

Perf events can open the door to processing all of the data that BPF exposes in novel and unexpected ways. We've shown you an example to inspire your imagination when you need to collect some kind of arbitrary data from the kernel; you can find many other examples in the tools that BCC provides for tracing.

Conclusion

In this chapter we've only scratched the surface of tracing with BPF. The Linux kernel gives you access to information that's more difficult to obtain with other tools. BPF makes this process more predictable because it provides a common interface to access this data. In later chapters you'll see more examples that use some of the techniques described here, such as attaching functions to tracepoints. They will help you cement what you've learned here.

We used the BCC framework in this chapter to write most of the examples. You can implement the same examples in C, like we did in previous chapters, but BCC provides several built-in features that make writing tracing programs much more accessible than C. If you're up for a fun challenge, try rewriting these examples in C.

In the next chapter, we show you some tools that the systems community has built on top of BPF to do performance analysis and tracing. Writing your own programs is powerful, but these dedicated tools give you access to much of the information we've seen here in packaged format. This way, you don't need to rewrite tools that already exist.

## CHAPTER 5

BPF Utilities

So far, we've talked about how you can write BPF programs to get more visibility within your systems. Over the years, many developers have built tools with BPF for that same purpose. In this chapter we talk about several of the off-the-shelf tools that you can use every day. Many of these tools are advanced versions of some BPF programs that you've already seen. Others are tools that will help you gain direct visibility into your own BPF programs.

This chapter covers some tools that will help you in your day-to-day work with BPF. We begin by covering BPFTool, a command-line utility to get more information about your BPF programs. We cover BPFTrace and kubectl-trace, which will help you write BPF programs more efficiently with a concise domain-specific language (DSL). Finally, we talk about eBPF Exporter, an open source project to integrate BPF with Prometheus.

BPFTool

BPFTool is a kernel utility for inspecting of BPF programs and maps. This tool doesn't come installed by default on any Linux distribution, and it's in heavy development, so you'll want to compile the version that best supports your Linux kernel. We cover the version of BPFTool distributed with version 5.1 of the Linux kernel.

In the next sections we discuss how to install BPFTool onto your system and how to use it to observe and change the behavior of your BPF programs and maps from the terminal.

Installation

To install BPFTool, you need to download a copy of the kernel's source code. There might be some packages for your specific Linux distribution online, but we're going to cover how to install it from the source because it's not too complicated.

1. Use Git to clone the repository from GitHub with `git clone https://github.com/torvalds/linux`.

2. Check out the specific kernel version tag with `git checkout v5.1`.

3. Within the kernel's source, navigate to the directory where BPFTool's source is stored with `cd tools/bpf/bpftool`.

4. Compile and install this tool with `make && sudo make install`.

You can check that BPFTool is correctly installed by checking its version:

```
# bpftool --version
bpftool v5.1.0
```

Feature Display

One of the basic operations that you can perform with BPFTool is scanning your system to know which BPF features you have access to. This is great when you don't remember which version of the kernel introduced which kind of programs or whether the BPF JIT compiler is enabled. To find out the answer to those questions, and many others, run this command:

```
# bpftool feature
```

You'll get some long output with details about all the supported BPF features in your systems. For brevity, we show you a cropped version of that output here:

```
Scanning system configuration...
bpf() syscall for unprivileged users is enabled
JIT compiler is enabled
...
Scanning eBPF program types...
eBPF program_type socket_filter is available
eBPF program_type kprobe is NOT available
...
Scanning eBPF map types...
eBPF map_type hash is available
eBPF map_type array is available
```

In this output you can see that our system allows unprivileged users to execute the syscall bpf, this call is restricted to certain operations. You can also see that the JIT is enabled. Newer versions of the kernel enable this JIT by default, and it helps greatly in compiling BPF programs. If your system doesn't have it enabled, you can run this command to enable it:

```
# echo 1 > /proc/sys/net/core/bpf_jit_enable
```

The feature output also shows you which program types and map types are enabled in your system. This command exposes much more information than what we're showing you here, like BPF helpers supported by program type and many other configuration directives. Feel free to dive into them while exploring your system.

Knowing what features you have at your disposal can be useful, especially if you need to dive into an unknown system. With that, we're ready to move on to other interesting BPFTool features, like inspecting loaded programs.

Inspecting BPF Programs

BPFTool gives you direct information about BPF programs on the kernel. It allows you to investigate what's already running in your system. It also allows you to load and pin new BPF programs that have been previously compiled from your command line.

The best starting point to learn how to use BPFTool to work with programs is by inspecting what you have running in your system. To do that, you can run the command `bpftool prog show`. If you're using Systemd as your init system, you probably already have a few BPF programs loaded and attached to some cgroups; we talk about these a little later. The output of running that command will look like this:

```
52: cgroup_skb  tag 7be49e3934a125ba
        loaded_at 2019-03-28T16:46:04-0700  uid 0
        xlated 296B  jited 229B  memlock 4096B  map_ids 52,53
53: cgroup_skb  tag 2a142ef67aaad174
        loaded_at 2019-03-28T16:46:04-0700  uid 0
        xlated 296B  jited 229B  memlock 4096B  map_ids 52,53
54: cgroup_skb  tag 7be49e3934a125ba
        loaded_at 2019-03-28T16:46:04-0700  uid 0
        xlated 296B  jited 229B  memlock 4096B  map_ids 54,55
```

The numbers on the left side, before the colon, are the program identifiers; we use them later to investigate what these programs are all about. From this output you can also learn which kinds of programs your system is running. In this case, the system is running three BPF programs attached to cgroup socket buffers. The loading time will likely match when you booted your system if those programs were actually started by Systemd. You can also see how much memory those programs are currently using and the identifiers for the maps associated with them. All of this is useful at first glance, and because we have the program identifiers, we can dive a little bit deeper.

You can add the program identifier to the previous command as an extra argument: `bpftool prog show id 52`. With that, BPFTool will show you the same information you saw before, but only for the program identified by the ID 52; that way, you can filter out information that you don't need. This command also supports a `--json` flag to generate some JSON output. This JSON output is very convenient if you want to manipulate the output. For example, tools like `jq` will give you a more structured formatting for this data:

```
# bpftool prog show --json id 52 | jq
{
  "id": 52,
  "type": "cgroup_skb",
  "tag": "7be49e3934a125ba",
  "gpl_compatible": false,
  "loaded_at": 1553816764,
  "uid": 0,
  "bytes_xlated": 296,
  "jited": true,
  "bytes_jited": 229,
  "bytes_memlock": 4096,
  "map_ids": [
    52,
    53
  ]
}
```

You can also perform more advanced manipulations and filter only the information that you're interested in. In the next example, we're interested only in knowing the BPF program identifier, which type of program it is, and when it was loaded in the kernel:

```
# bpftool prog show --json id 52 | jq -c '[.id, .type, .loaded_at]'
[52,"cgroup_skb",1553816764]
```

When you know a program identifier, you can also get a dump of the whole program using BPFTool; this can be handy when you need to debug the BPF bytecode generated by a compiler:

```
# bpftool prog dump xlated id 52
    0: (bf) r6 = r1
    1: (69) r7 = *(u16 *)(r6 +192)
    2: (b4) w8 = 0
    3: (55) if r7 != 0x8 goto pc+14
    4: (bf) r1 = r6
    5: (b4) w2 = 16
    6: (bf) r3 = r10
    7: (07) r3 += -4
    8: (b4) w4 = 4
    9: (85) call bpf_skb_load_bytes#7151872
    ...
```

This program loaded in our kernel by Systemd is inspecting packet data by using the helper `bpf_skb_load_bytes`.

If you want a more visual representation of this program, including instruction jumps, you can use the `visual` keyword in this command. That will generate the output in a format that you can convert to a graph representation with tools like `dotty`, or any other program that can draw graphs:

```
# bpftool prog dump xlated id 52 visual &> output.out
# dot -Tpng output.out -o visual-graph.png
```

You can see the visual representation for a small Hello World program in Figure 5-1.

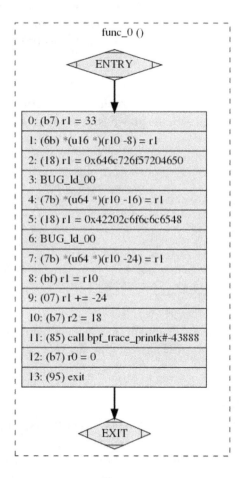

Figure 5-1. Visual representation of a BPF program

If you're running version 5.1 or newer of the kernel, you'll also have access to runtime statistics. They tell you how long the kernel is spending on your BPF programs. This feature might not be enabled in your system by default; you'll need to run this command first to let the kernel know that it needs to show you that data:

```
# sysctl -w kernel.bpf_stats_enabled=1
```

When the stats are enabled, you'll get two more pieces of information when you run BPFTool: the total amount of time that the kernel has spent running that program (run_time_ns), and how many times it has run it (run_cnt):

```
52: cgroup_skb  tag 7be49e3934a125ba  run_time_ns 14397 run_cnt 39
        loaded_at 2019-03-28T16:46:04-0700  uid 0
        xlated 296B  jited 229B  memlock 4096B  map_ids 52,53
```

But BPFTool doesn't only allow you to inspect how your programs are doing; it also lets you load new programs into the kernel and attach some of them to sockets and cgroups. For example, we can load one of our previous programs and pin it to the BPF file system, with this command:

```
# bpftool prog load bpf_prog.o /sys/fs/bpf/bpf_prog
```

Because the program is pinned to the filesystem, it won't terminate after running, and we can see that it's still loaded with the previous show command:

```
# bpftool prog show
52: cgroup_skb  tag 7be49e3934a125ba
        loaded_at 2019-03-28T16:46:04-0700  uid 0
        xlated 296B  jited 229B  memlock 4096B  map_ids 52,53
53: cgroup_skb  tag 2a142ef67aaad174
        loaded_at 2019-03-28T16:46:04-0700  uid 0
        xlated 296B  jited 229B  memlock 4096B  map_ids 52,53
54: cgroup_skb  tag 7be49e3934a125ba
        loaded_at 2019-03-28T16:46:04-0700  uid 0
        xlated 296B  jited 229B  memlock 4096B  map_ids 54,55
60: perf_event  name bpf_prog  tag c6e8e35bea53af79
        loaded_at 2019-03-28T20:46:32-0700  uid 0
        xlated 112B  jited 115B  memlock 4096B
```

As you can see, BPFTool gives you a lot of information about the programs loaded in your kernel without having to write and compile any code. Let's see how to work with BPF maps next.

Inspecting BPF Maps

Besides giving you access to inspect and manipulate BPF programs, BPFTool can give you access to the BPF maps that those programs are using. The command to list all maps and filter maps by their identifiers is similar to the show command that you saw previously. Instead of asking BPFTool to display information for prog, let's ask it to show us information for map:

```
# bpftool map show
52: lpm_trie  flags 0x1
        key 8B  value 8B  max_entries 1  memlock 4096B
53: lpm_trie  flags 0x1
        key 20B  value 8B  max_entries 1  memlock 4096B
```

```
54: lpm_trie  flags 0x1
        key 8B  value 8B  max_entries 1  memlock 4096B
55: lpm_trie  flags 0x1
        key 20B  value 8B  max_entries 1  memlock 4096B
```

Those maps match the identifiers that you saw earlier attached to your programs. You can also filter maps by their ID, in the same way we filtered programs by their ID earlier.

You can use BPFTool to create and update maps and to list all the elements within a map. Creating a new map requires the same information that you provide when you initialize a map along with one of your programs. We need to specify which type of map we want to create, the size of the keys and values, and its name. Because we're not initializing the map along with a program, we also need to pin it to the BPF filesystem so that we can use it later:

```
# bpftool map create /sys/fs/bpf/counter
    type array key 4 value 4 entries 5 name counter
```

If you list the maps in the system after running that command, you'll see the new map at the bottom of the list:

```
52: lpm_trie  flags 0x1
        key 8B  value 8B  max_entries 1  memlock 4096B
53: lpm_trie  flags 0x1
        key 20B  value 8B  max_entries 1  memlock 4096B
54: lpm_trie  flags 0x1
        key 8B  value 8B  max_entries 1  memlock 4096B
55: lpm_trie  flags 0x1
        key 20B  value 8B  max_entries 1  memlock 4096B
56: lpm_trie  flags 0x1
        key 8B  value 8B  max_entries 1  memlock 4096B
57: lpm_trie  flags 0x1
        key 20B  value 8B  max_entries 1  memlock 4096B
58: array  name counter  flags 0x0
        key 4B  value 4B  max_entries 5  memlock 4096B
```

After you've created the map, you can update and delete elements like we'd do inside a BPF program.

Remember that you cannot remove elements from fixed-size arrays; you can only update them. But you can totally delete elements from other maps, like hash maps.

If you want to add a new element to the map or update an existing one, you can use the map update command. You can grab the map identifier from the previous example:

```
# bpftool map update id 58 key 1 0 0 0 value 1 0 0 0
```

If you try to update an element with an invalid key or value, BPFTool will return an error:

```
# bpftool map update id 58 key 1 0 0 0 value 1 0 0
Error: value expected 4 bytes got 3
```

BPFTool can give you a dump of all the elements in a map if you need to inspect its values. You can see how BPF initializes all of the elements to a null value when you create fixed-size array maps:

```
# bpftool map dump id 58
key: 00 00 00 00  value: 00 00 00 00
key: 01 00 00 00  value: 01 00 00 00
key: 02 00 00 00  value: 00 00 00 00
key: 03 00 00 00  value: 00 00 00 00
key: 04 00 00 00  value: 00 00 00 00
```

One of the most powerful options that BPFTool gives you is that you can attach pre-created maps to new programs and replace the maps that they would initialize with those preallocated maps. That way, you can give programs access to saved data from the beginning, even if you didn't write the program to read a map from the BPF file system. To do that, you need to set the map you want to initialize when you load the program with BPFTool. You can specify the map by the ordered identifier that it would have when the program loads it, for example 0 for the first map, 1 for the second one, and so on. You can also specify the map by its name, which is usually more convenient:

```
# bpftool prog load bpf_prog.o /sys/fs/bpf/bpf_prog_2 \
    map name counter /sys/fs/bpf/counter
```

In this example we attach the map that we just created to a new program. In this case, we replace the map by its name, because we know that the program initializes a map called counter. You can also use the map's index position with the keyword idx, as in idx 0, if that's easier to remember for you.

Accessing BPF maps directly from the command line is useful when you need to debug message passing in real time. BPFTool gives you direct access in a convenient way. Besides introspecting programs and maps, you can use BPFTool to extract much more information from the kernel. Let's see how to access specific interfaces next.

Inspecting Programs Attached to Specific Interfaces

Sometimes you'll find yourself wondering which programs are attached to specific interfaces. BPF can load programs that work on top of cgroups, Perf events, and network packets. The subcommands cgroup, perf, and net can help you trace back attachments on those interfaces.

The perf subcommand lists all programs attached to tracing points in the system, like kprobes, uprobes, and tracepoints; you can see that listing by running bpftool perf show.

The net subcommand lists programs attached to XDP and Traffic Control. Other attachments, like socket filters and reuseport programs, are accessible only by using iproute2. You can list the attachments to XDP and TC with bpftool net show, like you've seen with other BPF objects.

Finally, the cgroup subcommand lists all programs attached to cgroups. This subcommand is a little bit different than the other ones you've seen. bpftool cgroup show requires the path to the cgroup you want to inspect. If you want to list all the attachments in all cgroups in the system, you'll need to use bpftool cgroup tree, as shown in this example:

```
# bpftool cgroup tree
CgroupPath
ID         AttachType      AttachFlags     Name
/sys/fs/cgroup/unified/system.slice/systemd-udevd.service
     5          ingress
     4          egress
/sys/fs/cgroup/unified/system.slice/systemd-journald.service
     3          ingress
     2          egress
/sys/fs/cgroup/unified/system.slice/systemd-logind.service
     7          ingress
     6          egress
```

Thanks to BPFTool, you can verify that your programs are attached correctly to any interface in the kernel, giving you quick visibility access to cgroups, Perf, and the network interface.

So far, we've talked about how you can enter different commands in your terminal to debug how your BPF programs behave. However, remembering all these commands can be cumbersome when you need them the most. Next we describe how to load several commands from plain-text files so that you can build a set of scripts that you can keep handy without having to retain each option that we've talked about.

Loading Commands in Batch Mode

It's common to run several commands over and over while you're trying to analyze the behavior of one or multiple systems. You might end up with a collection of commands that you use frequently as part of your toolchain. BPFTool's batch mode is for you if you don't want to type those commands every single time.

With batch mode, you can write all of the commands that you want to execute in a file and run all of them at once. You can also write comments in this file by starting a line with #. However, this execution mode is not atomic. BPFTool executes commands line by line, and it will abort the execution if one of the commands fails, leaving the system in the state it was in after running the latest successful command.

This is a short example of a file that batch mode can process:

```
# Create a new hash map
map create /sys/fs/bpf/hash_map type hash key 4 value 4 entries 5 name hash_map
# Now show all the maps in the system
map show
```

If you save those commands in a file called */tmp/batch_example.txt*, you'll be able to load it with `bpftool batch file /tmp/batch_example.txt`. You'll get output similar to the following snippet when you run this command for the first time, but if you try to run it again, the command will exit with no output because we already have a map with the name hash_map in the system, and the batch execution will fail in the first line:

```
# bpftool batch file /tmp/batch_example.txt
2: lpm_trie  flags 0x1
        key 8B   value 8B   max_entries 1   memlock 4096B
3: lpm_trie  flags 0x1
        key 20B  value 8B   max_entries 1   memlock 4096B
18: hash  name hash_map  flags 0x0
        key 4B   value 4B   max_entries 5   memlock 4096B
processed 2 commands
```

Batch mode is one of our favorite options in BPFTool. We recommend keeping these batch files in a version control system so that you can share them with your team to create your own set of utility tools. Before jumping to our next favorite utility, let's see how BPFTool can help you understand the BPF Type Format better.

Displaying BTF Information

BPFTool can display BPF Type Format (BTF) information for any given binary object when it is present. As we mentioned in Chapter 2, BTF annotates program structures with metadata information to help you debug programs.

For example, it can give you the source file and line numbers for each instruction in a BPF program when you add the keyword `linum` to `prog dump`.

More recent versions of BPFTool include a new `btf` subcommand to help you dive into your programs. The initial focus of this command is to visualize structure types. For example, `bpftool btf dump id 54` shows all of the BFT types for the program loaded with an ID of 54.

These are some of the things you can use BPFTool for. It's a low-friction entry point to any system, especially if you don't work on that system on a day-to-day basis.

BPFTrace

BPFTrace is a high-level tracing language for BPF. It allows you to write BPF programs with a concise DSL, and save them as scripts that you can execute without having to compile and load them in the kernel manually. The language is inspired by other well-known tools, like awk and DTrace. If you're familiar with DTrace and you've always missed being able to use it on Linux, you're going to find in BPFTrace a great substitute.

One of the advantages of using BPFTrace over writing programs directly with BCC or other BPF tooling is that BPFTrace provides a lot of built-in functionality that you don't need to implement yourself, such as aggregating information and creating histograms. On the other hand, the language that BPFTrace uses is much more limited, and it will get in your way if you try to implement advanced programs. In this section, we show you the most important aspects of the language. We recommend going to the BPFTrace repository on GitHub (*https://github.com/iovisor/bpftrace*) to learn about it.

Installation

You can install BPFTrace in several ways, although its developers recommend you use one of the prebuilt packages for your specific Linux distribution. They also maintain a document with all the installation options and prerequisites for your system in their repository. There, you'll find instructions in the installation document (*https://oreil.ly/h9Pha*).

Language Reference

The programs that BPFTrace executes have a terse syntax. We can divide them into three sections: header, action blocks, and footer. The header is a special block that BPFTrace executes when it loads the program; it's commonly used to print some information at the top of the output, like a preamble. In the same way, the footer is a special block that BPFTrace executes once before terminating the program. Both the header and footer are optional sections in a BPFTrace program. A BPFTrace program must have at least one *action block*. Action blocks are where we specify the probes that we want to trace and the actions we perform when the kernel fires the events for those probes. The next snippet shows you these three sections in a basic example:

```
BEGIN
{
  printf("starting BPFTrace program\n")
}

kprobe:do_sys_open
{
  printf("opening file descriptor: %s\n", str(arg1))
```

```
}

END
{
    printf("exiting BPFTrace program\n")
}
```

The header section is always marked with the keyword BEGIN, and the footer section is always marked with the keyword END. These keywords are reserved by BPFTrace. Action block identifiers define the probe to which you want to attach the BPF action. In the previous example, we printed a log line every time the kernel opens a file.

Besides identifying the program sections, we can already see a few more details about the language syntax in the previous examples. BPFTrace provides some helpers that are translated to BPF code when the program is compiled. The helper printf is a wrapper around the C function printf, which prints program details when you need it. str is a built-in helper that translates a C pointer to its string representation. Many kernel functions receive pointers to characters as arguments; this helper translates those pointers to strings for you.

BPFTrace could be considered a dynamic language in the sense that it doesn't know the number of arguments a probe might receive when it's executed by the kernel. This is why BPFTrace provides argument helpers to access the information that the kernel processes. BPFTrace generates these helpers dynamically depending on the number of arguments the block receives, and you can access the information by its position in the list of arguments. In the previous example, arg1 is the reference to the second argument in the open syscall, which makes reference to the file path.

To execute this example, you can save it in a file and run BPFTrace with the file path as the first argument:

```
# bpftrace /tmp/example.bt
```

BPFTrace's language is designed with scripting in mind. In the previous examples, you've seen the terse version of the language, so you can get familiar with it. But many of the programs that you can write with BPFTrace fit on one single line. You don't need to store those one-line programs in files to execute them; you can run them with the option -e when you execute BPFTrace. For example, the previous counter example can be a one-liner by collapsing the action block into a single line:

```
# bpftrace -e "kprobe:do_sys_open { @opens[str(arg1)] = count() }"
```

Now that you know a little bit more about BPFTrace's language, let's see how to use it in several scenarios.

Filtering

When you run the previous example, you probably get a stream of files that your system is constantly opening, until you press Ctrl-C to exit the program. That's because we're telling BPF to print every file descriptor that the kernel opens. There are situations when you want to execute the action block only for specific conditions. BPFTrace calls that *filtering*.

You can associate one filter to each action block. They are evaluated like action blocks, but the action does not execute if the filter returns a false value. They also have access to the rest of the language, including probe arguments and helpers. These filters are encapsulated within two slashes after the action header:

```
kprobe:do_sys_open /str(arg1) == "/tmp/example.bt"/
{
  printf("opening file descriptor: %s\n", str(arg1))
}
```

In this example, we refine our action block to be executed only when the file the kernel is opening is the file that we're using to store this example. If you run the program with the new filter, you'll see that it prints the header, but it stops printing there. This is because every file that was triggering our action before is being skipped now thanks to our new filter. If you open the example file several times in a different terminal, you'll see how the kernel executes the action when the filter matches our file path:

```
# bpftrace /tmp/example.bt
Attaching 3 probes...
starting BPFTrace program
opening file descriptor: /tmp/example.bt
opening file descriptor: /tmp/example.bt
opening file descriptor: /tmp/example.bt
^Cexiting BPFTrace program
```

BPFTrace's filtering capabilities are super helpful to hide information that you don't need, keeping data scoped to what you really care about. Next we talk about how BPFTrace makes working with maps seamless.

Dynamic Mapping

One handy feature that BPFTrace implements is dynamic map associations. It can generate BPF maps dynamically that you can use for many of the operations you've seen throughout the book. All map associations start with the character @, followed by the name of the map that you want to create. You can also associate update elements in those maps by assigning them values.

If we take the example that we started this section with, we could aggregate how often our system opens specific files. To do that, we need to count how many times the kernel runs the open syscall on a specific file, and then store those counters in a map. To identify those aggregations, we can use the file path as the map's key. This is how our action block would look in this case:

```
kprobe:do_sys_open
{
  @opens[str(arg1)] = count()
}
```

If you run your program again, you'll get output similar to this:

```
# bpftrace /tmp/example.bt
Attaching 3 probes...
starting BPFTrace program
^Cexiting BPFTrace program

@opens[/var/lib/snapd/lib/gl/haswell/libdl.so.2]: 1
@opens[/var/lib/snapd/lib/gl32/x86_64/libdl.so.2]: 1
...
@opens[/usr/lib/locale/en.utf8/LC_TIME]: 10
@opens[/usr/lib/locale/en_US/LC_TIME]: 10
@opens[/usr/share/locale/locale.alias]: 12
@opens[/proc/8483/cmdline]: 12
```

As you can see, BPFTrace prints the contents of the map when it stops the program execution. And as we expected, it's aggregating how often the kernel is opening the files in our system. By default, BPFTrace is always going to print the contents of every map it creates when it terminates. You don't need to specify that you want to print a map; it always assumes that you want to. You can change that behavior by clearing the map inside the END block by using the built-in function clear. This works because printing maps always happens after the footer block is executed.

BPFTrace dynamic mapping is super convenient. It removes a lot of boilerplate required to work with maps and focuses on helping you to collect data easily.

BPFTrace is a powerful tool for your day-to-day tasks. Its scripting language gives you enough flexibility to access every aspect of your system without the ceremony of having to compile and load your BPF program into the kernel manually, and this can help you trace and debug problems in your system from the get-go. Check out the reference guide in its GitHub repository to learn how to take advantage of all of its built-in capabilities, such as automatic histograms and stack trace aggregations.

In the next section we explore how to use BPFTrace inside Kubernetes.

kubectl-trace

kubectl-trace is a fantastic plug-in for the Kubernetes command line, kubectl. It helps you schedule BPFTrace programs in your Kubernetes cluster without having to install any additional packages or modules. It does this by scheduling a Kubernetes job with a container image that has everything you need to run the program installed already. This image is called `trace-runner`, and it's also available in the public Docker registry.

Installation

You need to install `kubectl-trace` from its source repository using Go's toolchain because its developers don't provide any binary package:

```
go get -u github.com/iovisor/kubectl-trace/cmd/kubectl-trace
```

kubectl's plug-in system will automatically detect this new add-on after Go's toolchain compiles the program and puts it in the path. `kubectl-trace` automatically downloads the Docker images that it needs to run in your cluster the first time that you execute it.

Inspecting Kubernetes Nodes

You can use `kubectl-trace` to target nodes and pods where containers run, and you can also use it to target processes running on those containers. In the first case, you can run pretty much any BPF program that you'd like. However, in the second case, you're restricted to running only the programs that attach user-space probes to those processes.

If you want to run a BPF program on a specific node, you need a proper identifier so that Kubernetes schedules the job in the appropriate place. After you have that identifier, running the program is similar to running the programs you saw earlier. This is how we would run our one-liner to count file openings:

```
# kubectl trace run node/node_identifier -e \
  "kprobe:do_sys_open { @opens[str(arg1)] = count() }"
```

As you can see, the program is exactly the same, but we're using the command `kubectl trace run` to schedule it in a specific cluster node. We use the syntax `node/...` to tell `kubectl-trace` that we're targetting a node in the cluster. If we want to target a specific pod, we'd replace `node/` with `pod/`.

Running a program on a specific container requires longer syntax; let's see an example first and go through it:

```
# kubectl trace run pod/pod_identifier -n application_name -e <<PROGRAM
uretprobe:/proc/$container_pid/exe:"main.main" {
  printf("exit: %d\n", retval)
}
PROGRAM
```

There are two interesting things to highlight in this command. The first is that we need the name of the application running in the container to be able to find its process; this corresponds with the `application_name` in our example. You'll want to use the name of the binary that's executed in the container, for example nginx or memc ached. Usually, containers run only one process, but this gives us extra guarantees that we're attaching our program to the correct process. The second aspect to high-light is the inclusion of $container_pid in our BPF program. This is not a BPFTrace helper, but a placeholder that kubectl-trace uses as a replacement for the process identifier. Before running the BPF program, the trace-runner substitutes the place-holder with the appropriate identifier, and it attaches our program to the correct process.

If you run Kubernetes in production, kubectl-trace will make your life much easier when you need to analyze your containers' behavior.

In this and the previous sections, we've focused on tools to help you run BPF pro-grams more efficiently, even within container environments. In the next section we talk about a nice tool to integrate data gathering from BPF programs with Prome-theus, a well-known open source monitoring system.

eBPF Exporter

eBPF Exporter is a tool that allows you to export custom BPF tracing metrics to Prometheus. Prometheus is a highly scalable monitoring and alerting system. One key factor that makes Prometheus different from other monitoring systems is that it uses a pull strategy to fetch metrics, instead of expecting the client to push metrics to it. This allows users to write custom exporters that can gather metrics from any sys-tem, and Prometheus will pull them using a well-defined API schema. eBPF Exporter implements this API to fetch tracing metrics from BPF programs and import them into Prometheus.

Installation

Although eBPF Exporter offers binary packages, we recommend installing it from source because there are often no new releases. Building from source also gives you access to newer functionality built on top of modern versions of BCC, the BPF Com-piler Collection.

To install eBPF Exporter from the source, you need to have BCC and Go's toolchain already installed on your computer. With those prerequisites, you can use Go to download and build the binary for you:

```
go get -u github.com/cloudflare/ebpf_exporter/...
```

Exporting Metrics from BPF

eBPF Exporter is configured using YAML files, in which you can specify the metrics that you want to collect from the system, the BPF program that generates those metrics, and how they translate to Prometheus. When Prometheus sends a request to eBPF Exporter to pull metrics, this tool translates the information that the BPF programs are collecting to metric values. Fortunately, eBPF Exporter bundles many programs that collect very useful information from your system, like instructions per cycle (IPC) and CPU cache hit rates.

A simple configuration file for eBPF Exporter includes three main sections. In the first section, you define the metrics that you want Prometheus to pull from the system. Here is where you translate the data collected in BPF maps to metrics that Prometheus understands. Following is an example of these translations from the project's examples:

```
programs:
  - name: timers
    metrics:
      counters:
        - name: timer_start_total
          help: Timers fired in the kernel
          table: counts
          labels:
            - name: function
              size: 8
              decoders:
                - name: ksym
```

We're defining a metric called `timer_start_total`, which aggregates how often the kernel starts a timer. We also specify that we want to collect this information from a BPF map called `counts`. Finally, we define a translation function for the map keys. This is necessary because map keys are usually pointers to the information, and we want to send Prometheus the actual function names.

The second section in this example describes the probes we want to attach our BPF program to. In this case, we want to trace the timer start calls; we use the tracepoint `timer:timer_start` for that:

```
tracepoints:
  timer:timer_start: tracepoint__timer__timer_start
```

Here we're telling eBPF Exporter that we want to attach the BPF function `trace point__timer__timer_start` to this specific tracepoint. Let's see how to declare that function next:

```
code: |
  BPF_HASH(counts, u64);
  // Generates function tracepoint__timer__timer_start
  TRACEPOINT_PROBE(timer, timer_start) {
      counts.increment((u64) args->function);
      return 0;
  }
```

The BPF program is inlined within the YAML file. This is probably one of our less favorite parts of this tool because YAML is particular about whitespacing, but it works for small programs like this one. eBPF Exporter uses BCC to compile programs, so we have access to all its macros and helpers. The previous snippet uses the macro `TRACEPOINT_PROBE` to generate the final function that we'll attach to our tracepoint with the name `tracepoint__timer__timer_start`.

Cloudflare uses eBPF Exporter to monitor metrics across all of its datacenters. The company made sure to bundle the most common metrics that you'll want to export from your systems. But as you can see, it's relatively easy to extend with new metrics.

Conclusion

In this chapter we talked about some of the our favorite tools for system analysis. These tools are general enough to have them on hand when you need to debug any kind of anomaly on your system. As you can see, all these tools abstract the concepts that we saw in the previous chapters to help you use BPF even when the environment is not ready for it. This is one of the many advantages of BPF before other analysis tools; because any modern Linux kernel includes the BPF VM, you can build new tools on top that take advantage of these powerful capabilities.

There are many other tools that use BPF for similar purposes, such as Cilium and Sysdig, and we encourage you to try them.

This chapter and Chapter 4 dealt mostly with system analysis and tracing, but there is much more that you can do with BPF. In the next chapters we dive into its networking capabilities. We show you how to analyze traffic in any network and how to use BPF to control messages in your network.

## CHAPTER 6

Linux Networking and BPF

From a networking point of view, we use BPF programs for two main use cases: packet capturing and filtering.

This means that a user-space program can attach a filter to any socket and extract information about packets flowing through it and allow/disallow/redirect certain kinds of packets as they are seen at that level.

The goal of this chapter is to explain how BPF programs can interact with the Socket Buffer structure at different stages of the network data path in the Linux kernel network stack. We are identifying, as common use cases two types of programs:

- Program types related to *sockets*
- Programs written for the BPF-based classifier for *Traffic Control*

The Socket Buffer structure, also called SKB or sk_buff, is the one in the kernel that is created and used for every packet sent or received. By reading the SKB you can pass or drop packets and populate BPF maps to create statistics and flow metrics about the current traffic.

In addition some BPF programs allow you to manipulate the SKB and, by extension, transform the final packets in order to redirect them or change their fundamental structure. For example, on an IPv6-only system, you might write a program that converts all the received packets from IPv4 to IPv6, which can be accomplished by mangling with the packets' SKB.

Understanding the differences between the different kinds of programs we can write and how different programs lead to the same goal is the key to understanding BPF and eBPF in networking; in the next section we look at the first two ways to do filtering at socket level: by using classic BPF filters, and by using eBPF programs attached to sockets.

BPF and Packet Filtering

As stated, BPF filters and eBPF programs are the principal use cases for BPF programs in the context of networking; however, originally, BPF programs were synonymous with packet filtering.

Packet filtering is still one of the most important use cases and has been expanded from classic BPF (cBPF) to the modern eBPF in Linux 3.19 with the addition of map-related functions to the filter program type `BPF_PROG_TYPE_SOCKET_FILTER`.

Filters can be used mainly in three high-level scenarios:

- Live traffic dropping (e.g., allowing only User Datagram Protocol [UDP] traffic and discarding anything else)
- Live observation of a filtered set of packets flowing into a live system
- Retrospective analysis of network traffic captured on a live system, using the *pcap format*, for example

 The term *pcap* comes from the conjunction of two words: packet and capture. The pcap format is implemented as a domain-specific API for packet capturing in a library called Packet Capture Library (*libpcap*). This format is useful in debugging scenarios when you want to save a set of packets that have been captured on a live system directly to a file to analyze them later using a tool that can read a stream of packets exported in the pcap format.

In the following sections we show two different ways to apply the concept of packet filtering with BPF programs. First we show how a common and widespread tool like `tcpdump` acts as a higher-level interface for BPF programs used as filters. Then we write and load our own program using the `BPF_PROG_TYPE_SOCKET_FILTER` BPF program type.

tcpdump and BPF Expressions

When talking about live traffic analysis and observation, one of the command-line tools that almost everyone knows about is `tcpdump`. Essentially a frontend for `libp cap`, it allows the user to define high-level filtering expressions. What `tcpdump` does is read packets from a network interface of your choice (or any interface) and then writes the content of the packets it received to stdout or a file. The packet stream can then be filtered using the pcap filter syntax. The pcap filter syntax is a DSL that is used to filter packets using a higher-level set of expressions made by a set of primitives that are generally easier to remember than BPF assembly. It's out of the scope of this chapter to explain all the primitives and expressions possible in the pcap filter syntax because the entire set can be found in `man 7 pcap-filter`, but we do go through some examples so that you can understand its power.

The scenario is that we are in a Linux box that is exposing a web server on port 8080; this web server is not logging the requests it receives, and we really want to know whether it is receiving any request and how those requests are flowing into it because a customer of the served application is complaining about not being able to get any response while browsing the products page. At this point, we know only that the customer is connecting to one of our products pages using our web application served by that web server, and as almost always happens, we have no idea what could be the cause of that because end users generally don't try to debug your services for you, and unfortunately we didn't deploy any logging or error reporting strategy into this system, so we are completely blind while investigating the problem. Fortunately, there's a tool that can come to our rescue! It is `tcpdump`, which can be told to filter only IPv4 packets flowing in our system that are using the Transmission Control Protocol (TCP) on port 8080. Therefore, we will be able to analyze the traffic of the web server and understand what are the faulty requests.

Here's the command to conduct that filtering with `tcpdump`:

```
# tcpdump -n 'ip and tcp port 8080'
```

Let's take a look at what's happening in this command:

- `-n` is there to tell `tcpdump` to not convert addresses to the respective names, we want to see the addresses for source and destination.
- `ip and tcp port 8080` is the pcap filter expression that `tcpdump` will use to filter your packets. `ip` means IPv4, `and` is a conjunction to express a more complex filter to allow adding more expressions to match, and then we specify that we are interested only in TCP packets coming from or to port 8080 using `tcp port 8080`. In this specific case a better filter would've been `tcp dst port 8080` because we are interested only in packets having as the destination port 8080 and not packets coming from it.

The output of that will be something like this (without the redundant parts like complete TCP handshakes):

```
tcpdump: verbose output suppressed, use -v or -vv for full protocol decode
listening on wlp4s0, link-type EN10MB (Ethernet), capture size 262144 bytes
12:04:29.593703 IP 192.168.1.249.44206 > 192.168.1.63.8080: Flags [P.],
    seq 1:325, ack 1, win 343,
    options [nop,nop,TS val 25580829 ecr 595195678],
```

```
          length 324: HTTP: GET / HTTP/1.1
12:04:29.596073 IP 192.168.1.63.8080 > 192.168.1.249.44206: Flags [.],
          seq 1:1449, ack 325, win 507,
          options [nop,nop,TS val 595195731 ecr 25580829],
          length 1448: HTTP: HTTP/1.1 200 OK
12:04:29.596139 IP 192.168.1.63.8080 > 192.168.1.249.44206: Flags [P.],
          seq 1449:2390, ack 325, win 507,
          options [nop,nop,TS val 595195731 ecr 25580829],
          length 941: HTTP
12:04:46.242924 IP 192.168.1.249.44206 > 192.168.1.63.8080: Flags [P.],
          seq 660:996, ack 4779, win 388,
          options [nop,nop,TS val 25584934 ecr 595204802],
          length 336: HTTP: GET /api/products HTTP/1.1
12:04:46.243594 IP 192.168.1.63.8080 > 192.168.1.249.44206: Flags [P.],
          seq 4779:4873, ack 996, win 503,
          options [nop,nop,TS val 595212378 ecr 25584934],
          length 94: HTTP: HTTP/1.1 500 Internal Server Error
12:04:46.329245 IP 192.168.1.249.44234 > 192.168.1.63.8080: Flags [P.],
          seq 471:706, ack 4779, win 388,
          options [nop,nop,TS val 25585013 ecr 595205622],
          length 235: HTTP: GET /favicon.ico HTTP/1.1
12:04:46.331659 IP 192.168.1.63.8080 > 192.168.1.249.44234: Flags [.],
          seq 4779:6227, ack 706, win 506,
          options [nop,nop,TS val 595212466 ecr 25585013],
          length 1448: HTTP: HTTP/1.1 200 OK
12:04:46.331739 IP 192.168.1.63.8080 > 192.168.1.249.44234: Flags [P.],
          seq 6227:7168, ack 706, win 506,
          options [nop,nop,TS val 595212466 ecr 25585013],
          length 941: HTTP
```

The situation is a lot clearer now! We have a bunch of requests going well, returning a 200 OK status code, but there is also one with a 500 Internal Server Error code on the /api/products endpoint. Our customer is right; we have a problem listing the products!

At this point, you might ask yourself, what does all this pcap filtering stuff and tcpdump have to do with BPF programs if they have their own syntax? Pcap filters on Linux are compiled to BPF programs! And because tcpdump uses pcap filters for the filtering, this means that every time you execute tcpdump using a filter, you are actually compiling and loading a BPF program to filter your packets. Fortunately, by passing the -d flag to tcpdump, you can dump the BPF instructions that it will load while using the specified filter:

```
tcpdump -d 'ip and tcp port 8080'
```

The filter is the same as the one used in the previous example, but the output now is a set of BPF assembly instructions because of the -d flag.

Here's the output:

```
(000) ldh      [12]
(001) jeq      #0x800          jt 2    jf 12
(002) ldb      [23]
(003) jeq      #0x6            jt 4    jf 12
(004) ldh      [20]
(005) jset     #0x1fff         jt 12   jf 6
(006) ldxb     4*([14]&0xf)
(007) ldh      [x + 14]
(008) jeq      #0x1f90         jt 11   jf 9
(009) ldh      [x + 16]
(010) jeq      #0x1f90         jt 11   jf 12
(011) ret      #262144
(012) ret      #0
```

Let's analyze it:

ldh [12]

(ld) Load a (h) half-word (16 bit) from the accumulator at offset 12, which is the Ethertype field, as shown in Figure 6-1.

jeq #0x800 jt 2 jf 12

(j) Jump if (eq) equal; check whether the Ethertype value from the previous instruction is equal to 0x800—which is the identifier for IPv4—and then use the jump destinations that are 2 if true (jt) and 12 if false (jf), so this will continue to the next instruction if the Internet Protocol is IPv4—otherwise it will jump to the end and return zero.

ldb [23]

Load byte into (ldb), will load the higher-layer protocol field from the IP frame that can be found at offset 23—offset 23 comes from the addition of the 14 bytes of the headers in the Ethernet Layer 2 frame (see Figure 6-1) plus the position the protocol has in the IPv4 header, which is the 9th, so 14 + 9 = 23.

jeq #0x6 jt 4 jf 12

Again a jump if equal. In this case, we check that the previous extracted protocol is 0 x 6, which is TCP. If it is, we jump to the next instruction (4) or we go to the end (12)—if it is not, we drop the packet.

ldh [20]

This is another load half-word instruction—in this case, it is to load the value of packet offset + fragment offset from the IPv4 header.

jset #0x1fff jt 12 6

This jset instruction will jump to 12 if any of the data we found in the fragment offset is true—otherwise, go to 6, which is the next instruction. The offset after the instruction 0x1fff says to the jset instruction to look only at the last 13 bytes of data. (Expanded it becomes 0001 1111 1111 1111.)

```
ldxb 4*([14]&0xf)
```
(ld) Load into x (x) what (b) is. This instruction will load the value of the IP header length into x.

```
ldh [x + 14]
```
Another load half-word instruction that will go get the value at offset (x + 14), IP header length + 14, which is the location of the source port within the packet.

```
jeq #0x1f90 jt 11 jf 9
```
If the value at (x + 14) is equal to 0x1f90 (8080 in decimal), which means that the source port will be 8080, continue to 11 or go check whether the destination is on port 8080 by continuing to 9 if this is false.

```
ldh [x + 16]
```
This is another load half-word instruction that will go get the value at offset (x + 16), which is the location of destination port in the packet.

```
jeq #0x1f90 jt 11 jf 12
```
Here's another jump if equal, this time used to check if the destination is 8080, go to 11; if not, go to 12 and discard the packet.

```
ret #262144
```
When this instruction is reached, a match is found—thus return the matched snap length. By default this value is 262,144 bytes. It can be tuned using the -s parameter in tcpdump.

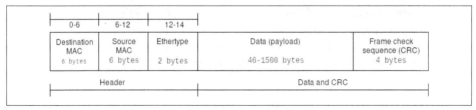

Figure 6-1. Layer 2 Ethernet frame structure

Here's the "correct" example because, as we said in the case of our web server, we only need to take into account the packet having 8080 as a destination, not as a source, so the tcpdump filter can specify it with the dst destination field:

```
tcpdump -d 'ip and tcp dst port 8080'
```

In this case, the dumped set of instructions is similar to the previous example, but as you can see, it lacks the entire part about matching the packets with a source of port 8080. In fact, there's no ldh [x + 14] and the relative jeq #0x1f90 jt 11 jf 9.

```
(000) ldh      [12]
(001) jeq      #0x800           jt 2   jf 10
```

```
(002) ldb       [23]
(003) jeq       #0x6              jt 4     jf 10
(004) ldh       [20]
(005) jset      #0x1fff           jt 10    jf 6
(006) ldxb      4*([14]&0xf)
(007) ldh       [x + 16]
(008) jeq       #0x1f90           jt 9     jf 10
(009) ret       #262144
(010) ret       #0
```

Besides just analyzing the generated assembly from tcpdump, as we did, you might want to write your own code to filter network packets. It turns out that the biggest challenge in that case would be to actually debug the execution of the code to make sure it matches our expectations; in this case, in the kernel source tree, there's a tool in tools/bpf called bpf_dbg.c that is essentially a debugger that allows you to load a program and a pcap file to test the execution step by step.

 tcpdump can also read directly from a .pcap file and apply BPF filters to it.

Packet Filtering for Raw Sockets

The BPF_PROG_TYPE_SOCKET_FILTER program type allows you to attach the BPF program to a socket. All of the packets received by it will be passed to the program in the form of an sk_buff struct, and then the program can decide whether to discard or allow them. This kind of programs also has the ability to access and work on maps.

Let's look at an example to see how this kind of BPF program can be used.

The purpose of our example program is to count the number of TCP, UDP, and Internet Control Message Protocol (ICMP) packets flowing in the interface under observation. To do that, we need the following:

- The BPF program that can see the packets flowing
- The code to load the program and attach it to a network interface
- A script to compile the program and launch the loader

At this point, we can write our BPF program in two ways: as C code that is then compiled to an *ELF* file, or directly as a BPF assembly. For this example, we opted to use C code to show a higher-level abstraction and how to use Clang to compile the program. It's important to note that to make this program, we are using headers and helpers available only in the Linux kernel's source tree, so the first thing to do is to obtain a copy of it using Git. To avoid differences, you can check out the same commit SHA we've used to make this example:

```
export KERNEL_SRCTREE=/tmp/linux-stable
git clone  git://git.kernel.org/pub/scm/linux/kernel/git/stable/linux-stable.git
  $KERNEL_SRCTREE
cd $KERNEL_SRCTREE
git checkout 4b3c31c8d4dda4d70f3f24a165f3be99499e0328
```

 To contain BPF support, you will need clang >= 3.4.0 with llvm >= 3.7.1. To verify BPF support in your installation, you can use the command llc -version and look to see whether it has the BPF target.

Now that you understand socket filtering, we can get our hands on a BPF program of type socket.

The BPF program

The main duty of the BPF program here is to access the packet it receives; check whether its protocol is TCP, UDP, or ICMP, and then increment the counter on the map array on the specific key for the found protocol.

For this program we are going to take advantage of the loading mechanism that parses *ELF* files using the helpers located in *samples/bpf/bpf_load.c* in the kernel source tree. The load function load_bpf_file is able to recognize some specific ELF section headers and can associate them to the respective program types. Here's how that code looks:

```
bool is_socket = strncmp(event, "socket", 6) == 0;
bool is_kprobe = strncmp(event, "kprobe/", 7) == 0;
bool is_kretprobe = strncmp(event, "kretprobe/", 10) == 0;
bool is_tracepoint = strncmp(event, "tracepoint/", 11) == 0;
bool is_raw_tracepoint = strncmp(event, "raw_tracepoint/", 15) == 0;
bool is_xdp = strncmp(event, "xdp", 3) == 0;
bool is_perf_event = strncmp(event, "perf_event", 10) == 0;
bool is_cgroup_skb = strncmp(event, "cgroup/skb", 10) == 0;
bool is_cgroup_sk = strncmp(event, "cgroup/sock", 11) == 0;
bool is_sockops = strncmp(event, "sockops", 7) == 0;
bool is_sk_skb = strncmp(event, "sk_skb", 6) == 0;
bool is_sk_msg = strncmp(event, "sk_msg", 6) == 0;
```

The first thing that the code does is to create an association between the section header and an internal variable—like for SEC("socket"), we will end up with bool is_socket=true.

Later in the same file, we see a set of if instructions that create the association between the header and the actual prog_type , so for is_socket, we end up with BPF_PROG_TYPE_SOCKET_FILTER:

```
if (is_socket) {
        prog_type = BPF_PROG_TYPE_SOCKET_FILTER;
} else if (is_kprobe || is_kretprobe) {
        prog_type = BPF_PROG_TYPE_KPROBE;
} else if (is_tracepoint) {
        prog_type = BPF_PROG_TYPE_TRACEPOINT;
} else if (is_raw_tracepoint) {
        prog_type = BPF_PROG_TYPE_RAW_TRACEPOINT;
} else if (is_xdp) {
        prog_type = BPF_PROG_TYPE_XDP;
} else if (is_perf_event) {
        prog_type = BPF_PROG_TYPE_PERF_EVENT;
} else if (is_cgroup_skb) {
        prog_type = BPF_PROG_TYPE_CGROUP_SKB;
} else if (is_cgroup_sk) {
        prog_type = BPF_PROG_TYPE_CGROUP_SOCK;
} else if (is_sockops) {
        prog_type = BPF_PROG_TYPE_SOCK_OPS;
} else if (is_sk_skb) {
        prog_type = BPF_PROG_TYPE_SK_SKB;
} else if (is_sk_msg) {
        prog_type = BPF_PROG_TYPE_SK_MSG;
} else {
        printf("Unknown event '%s'\n", event);
        return -1;
}
```

Good, so because we want to write a BPF_PROG_TYPE_SOCKET_FILTER program, we need to specify a SEC("socket") as an ELF header to our function that will act as an entry point for our BPF program.

As you can see by that list, there are a variety of program types related to sockets and in general network operations. In this chapter we are showing examples with BPF_PROG_TYPE_SOCKET_FILTER; however, you can find a definition of all the other program types in Chapter 2. Moreover, in Chapter 7 we discuss XDP programs with the program type BPF_PROG_TYPE_XDP.

Because we want to store the count of packets for every protocol we encounter, we need to create a key/value map where the protocol is key and the packets count as value. For that purpose, we can use a BPF_MAP_TYPE_ARRAY:

```
struct bpf_map_def SEC("maps") countmap = {
    .type = BPF_MAP_TYPE_ARRAY,
    .key_size = sizeof(int),
    .value_size = sizeof(int),
    .max_entries = 256,
};
```

The map is defined using the `bpf_map_def` struct, and it will be named `countmap` for reference in the program.

At this point, we can write some code to actually count the packets. We know that programs of type `BPF_PROG_TYPE_SOCKET_FILTER` are one of our options because by using such a program, we can see all the packets flowing through an interface. Therefore we attach the program to the right header with `SEC("socket")`:

```
SEC("socket")
int socket_prog(struct __sk_buff *skb) {
  int proto = load_byte(skb, ETH_HLEN + offsetof(struct iphdr, protocol));
  int one = 1;
  int *el = bpf_map_lookup_elem(&countmap, &proto);
  if (el) {
    (*el)++;
  } else {
    el = &one;
  }
  bpf_map_update_elem(&countmap, &proto, el, BPF_ANY);
  return 0;
}
```

After the ELF header attachment we can use the `load_byte` function to extract the protocol section from the `sk_buff` struct. Then we use the protocol ID as a key to do a `bpf_map_lookup_elem` operation to extract the current counter value from our `countmap` so that we can increment it or set it to 1 if it is the first packet ever. Now we can update the map with the incremented value using `bpf_map_update_elem`.

To compile the program to an *ELF* file, we just use Clang with `-target bpf`. This command creates a `bpf_program.o` file that we will load using the loader:

```
clang -O2 -target bpf -c bpf_program.c -o bpf_program.o
```

Load and attach to a network interface

The loader is the program that actually opens our compiled BPF ELF binary `bpf_pro`
`gram.o` and attaches the defined BPF program and its maps to a socket that is created against the interface under observation, in our case `lo`, the loopback interface.

The most important part of the loader is the actual loading of the *ELF* file:

```
if (load_bpf_file(filename)) {
  printf("%s", bpf_log_buf);
  return 1;
}

sock = open_raw_sock("lo");

if (setsockopt(sock, SOL_SOCKET, SO_ATTACH_BPF, prog_fd,
               sizeof(prog_fd[0]))) {
  printf("setsockopt %s\n", strerror(errno));
```

```
    return 0;
}
```

This will populate the `prog_fd` array by adding one element that is the file descriptor of our loaded program that we can now attach to the socket descriptor of our loopback interface `lo` opened with `open_raw_sock`.

The attach is done by setting the option `SO_ATTACH_BPF` to the raw socket opened for the interface.

At this point our user-space loader is able to look up map elements while the kernel sends them:

```
for (i = 0; i < 10; i++) {
    key = IPPROTO_TCP;
    assert(bpf_map_lookup_elem(map_fd[0], &key, &tcp_cnt) == 0);

    key = IPPROTO_UDP;
    assert(bpf_map_lookup_elem(map_fd[0], &key, &udp_cnt) == 0);

    key = IPPROTO_ICMP;
    assert(bpf_map_lookup_elem(map_fd[0], &key, &icmp_cnt) == 0);

    printf("TCP %d UDP %d ICMP %d packets\n", tcp_cnt, udp_cnt, icmp_cnt);
    sleep(1);
}
```

To do the lookup, we attach to the array map using a `for` loop and `bpf_map_lookup_elem` so that we can read and print the values for the TCP, UDP, and ICMP packet counters, respectively.

The only thing left is to compile the program!

Because this program is using *libbpf*, we need to compile it from the kernel source tree we just cloned:

```
$ cd $KERNEL_SRCTREE/tools/lib/bpf
$ make
```

Now that we have *libbpf*, we can compile the loader using this script:

```
KERNEL_SRCTREE=$1
LIBBPF=${KERNEL_SRCTREE}/tools/lib/bpf/libbpf.a
clang -o loader-bin -I${KERNEL_SRCTREE}/tools/lib/bpf/ \
  -I${KERNEL_SRCTREE}/tools/lib -I${KERNEL_SRCTREE}/tools/include \
  -I${KERNEL_SRCTREE}/tools/perf -I${KERNEL_SRCTREE}/samples \
  ${KERNEL_SRCTREE}/samples/bpf/bpf_load.c \
  loader.c "${LIBBPF}" -lelf
```

As you can see, the script includes a bunch of headers and the *libbpf* library from the kernel itself, so it must know where to find the kernel source code. To do that, you can replace $KERNEL_SRCTREE in it or just write that script into a file and use it:

```
$ ./build-loader.sh /tmp/linux-stable
```

At this point the loader will have created a loader-bin file that can be finally started along with the BPF program's *ELF* file (requires root privileges):

```
# ./loader-bin bpf_program.o
```

After the program is loaded and started it will do 10 dumps, one every second showing the packet count for each one of the three considered protocols. Because the program is attached to the loopback device lo, along with the loader you can run ping and see the ICMP counter increasing.

So run ping to generate ICMP traffic to localhost:

```
$ ping -c 100 127.0.0.1
```

This starts pinging localhost 100 times and outputs something like this:

```
PING 127.0.0.1 (127.0.0.1) 56(84) bytes of data.
64 bytes from 127.0.0.1: icmp_seq=1 ttl=64 time=0.100 ms
64 bytes from 127.0.0.1: icmp_seq=2 ttl=64 time=0.107 ms
64 bytes from 127.0.0.1: icmp_seq=3 ttl=64 time=0.093 ms
64 bytes from 127.0.0.1: icmp_seq=4 ttl=64 time=0.102 ms
64 bytes from 127.0.0.1: icmp_seq=5 ttl=64 time=0.105 ms
64 bytes from 127.0.0.1: icmp_seq=6 ttl=64 time=0.093 ms
64 bytes from 127.0.0.1: icmp_seq=7 ttl=64 time=0.104 ms
64 bytes from 127.0.0.1: icmp_seq=8 ttl=64 time=0.142 ms
```

Then, in another terminal, we can finally run our BPF program:

```
# ./loader-bin bpf_program.o
```

It begins dumping out the following:

```
TCP 0 UDP 0 ICMP 0 packets
TCP 0 UDP 0 ICMP 4 packets
TCP 0 UDP 0 ICMP 8 packets
TCP 0 UDP 0 ICMP 12 packets
TCP 0 UDP 0 ICMP 16 packets
TCP 0 UDP 0 ICMP 20 packets
TCP 0 UDP 0 ICMP 24 packets
TCP 0 UDP 0 ICMP 28 packets
TCP 0 UDP 0 ICMP 32 packets
TCP 0 UDP 0 ICMP 36 packets
```

At this point, you already know a good amount of what is needed to filter packets on Linux using a socket filter eBPF program. Here's some big news: that's not the only way! You might want to instrument the packet scheduling subsystem in place by using the kernel instead of on sockets directly. Just read the next section to learn how.

BPF-Based Traffic Control Classifier

Traffic Control is the kernel packet scheduling subsystem architecture. It is made of mechanisms and queuing systems that can decide how packets flow and how they are accepted.

Some use cases for Traffic Control include, but are not limited to, the following:

- Prioritize certain kinds of packets
- Drop specific kind of packet
- Bandwidth distribution

Given that in general Traffic Control is the way to go when you need to redistribute network resources in a system, to get the best out of it, specific Traffic Control configurations should be deployed based on the kind of applications that you want to run. Traffic Control provides a programmable classifier, called `cls_bpf`, to let the hook into different levels of the scheduling operations where they can read and update socket buffer and packet metadata to do things like traffic shaping, tracing, preprocessing, and more.

Support for eBPF in `cls_bpf` was implemented in kernel 4.1, which means that this kind of program has access to eBPF maps, has tail call support, can access IPv4/IPv6 tunnel metadata, and in general use helpers and utilities coming with eBPF.

The tooling used to interact with networking configuration related to Traffic Control is part of the iproute2 (*https://oreil.ly/SYGwI*) suite, which contains `ip` and `tc`, which are used to manipulate network interfaces and traffic control configuration, respectively.

At this point, learning Traffic Control can be difficult without the proper reference in terms of terminology. The following section can help.

Terminology

As mentioned, there are interaction points between Traffic Control and BPF programs, so you need to understand some Traffic Control concepts. If you have already mastered Traffic Control, feel free to skip this terminology section and go straight to the examples.

Queueing disciplines

Queuing disciplines (qdisc) define the scheduling objects used to enqueue packets going to an interface by changing the way they are sent; those objects can be classless or classful.

The default qdisc is `pfifo_fast`, which is classless and enqueues packets on three FIFO (first in first out) queues that are dequeued based on their priority; this qdisc is not used for virtual devices like the loopback (`lo`) or Virtual Ethernet devices (`veth`) that use `noqueue` instead. Besides being a good default for its scheduling algorithm, `pfifo_fast` also doesn't require any configuration to work.

Virtual interfaces can be distinguished from physical interfaces (devices) by asking the */sys* pseudo filesystem:

```
ls -la /sys/class/net
total 0
drwxr-xr-x  2 root root 0 Feb 13 21:52 .
drwxr-xr-x 64 root root 0 Feb 13 18:38 ..
lrwxrwxrwx  1 root root 0 Feb 13 23:26 docker0 ->
../../devices/virtual/net/docker0
lrwxrwxrwx  1 root root 0 Feb 13 23:26 enp0s31f6 ->
../../devices/pci0000:00/0000:00:1f.6/net/enp0s31f6
lrwxrwxrwx  1 root root 0 Feb 13 23:26 lo -> ../../devices/virtual/net/lo
```

At this point, some confusion is normal. If you've never heard about qdiscs, one thing you can do is to use the `ip a` command to show the list of network interfaces configured in the current system:

```
ip a
1: lo: <LOOPBACK,UP,LOWER_UP> mtu 65536 qdisc noqueue
state UNKNOWN group default qlen 1000
    link/loopback 00:00:00:00:00:00 brd 00:00:00:00:00:00
    inet 127.0.0.1/8 scope host lo
    valid_lft forever preferred_lft forever
    inet6 ::1/128 scope host
    valid_lft forever preferred_lft forever
2: enp0s31f6: <NO-CARRIER,BROADCAST,MULTICAST,UP> mtu 1500 qdisc
fq_codel stateDOWN group default
qlen 1000
link/ether 8c:16:45:00:a7:7e brd ff:ff:ff:ff:ff:ff
6: docker0: <NO-CARRIER,BROADCAST,MULTICAST,UP> mtu 1500 qdisc
noqueue state DOWN group default
link/ether 02:42:38:54:3c:98 brd ff:ff:ff:ff:ff:ff
inet 172.17.0.1/16 brd 172.17.255.255 scope global docker0
   valid_lft forever preferred_lft forever
inet6 fe80::42:38ff:fe54:3c98/64 scope link
   valid_lft forever preferred_lft forever
```

This list already tells us something. Can you find the word qdisc in it? Let's analyze the situation:

- We have three network interfaces in this system: `lo`, `enp0s31f6`, and `docker0`.

- The `lo` interface is a virtual interface, so it has qdisc `noqueue`.

- The `enp0s31f6` is a physical interface. Wait, why is the qdisc here `fq_codel` (fair queue controlled delay)? Wasn't `pfifo_fast` the default? It turns out that the system we're testing the commands on is running Systemd, which is setting the default qdisc differently using the kernel parameter `net.core.default_qdisc`.

- The `docker0` interface is a bridge interface, so it uses a `virtual` device and has `noqueue` qdisc.

The `noqueue` qdisc doesn't have classes, a scheduler, or a classifier. What it does is that it tries to send the packets immediately. As stated, `noqueue` is used by default by virtual devices, but it's also the qdisc that becomes effective to any interface when you delete its current associated qdisc.

`fq_codel` is a classless qdisc that classifies the incoming packets using a stochastic model in order to be able to queue traffic flows in a fair way.

The situation should be clearer now; we used the `ip` command to find information about `qdiscs` but it turns out that in the `iproute2` toolbelt there's also a tool called `tc` that has a specific subcommand for qdiscs you can use to list them:

```
tc qdisc ls
qdisc noqueue 0: dev lo root refcnt 2
qdisc fq_codel 0: dev enp0s31f6 root refcnt 2 limit 10240p flows 1024 quantum 1514
target 5.0ms interval 100.0ms memory_limit 32Mb ecn
qdisc noqueue 0: dev docker0 root refcnt 2
```

There's much more going on here! For `docker0` and `lo` we basically see the same information as with `ip a`, but for `enp0s31f6`, for example, it has the following:

- A limit of 10,240 incoming packets that it can handle.

- As mentioned, the stochastic model used by `fq_codel` wants to queue traffic into different flows, and this output contains the information about how many of them we have, which is 1,024.

Now that the key concepts of qdiscs have been introduced, we can take a closer look at classful and classless qdiscs in the next section to understand their differences and which ones are suitable for BPF programs.

Classful qdiscs, filters, and classes

Classful qdiscs allow the definition of classes for different kinds of traffic in order to apply different rules to them. Having a class for a qdisc means that it can contain further qdiscs. With this kind of hieararchy, then, we can use a filter (classifier) to classify the traffic by determining the next class where the packet should be enqueued.

Filters are used to assign packets to a particular class based on their type. Filters are used inside a classful qdiscs to determine in which class the packet should be enqueued, and two or more filters can map to the same class, as shown in Figure 6-2. Every filter uses a classifier to classify packets based on their information.

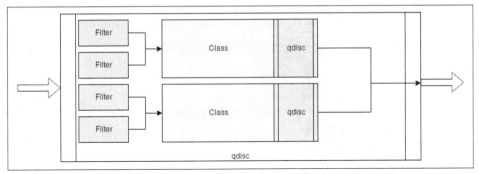

Figure 6-2. Classful qdisc with filters

As mentioned earlier, cls_bpf is the classifier that we want to use to write BPF programs for Traffic Control—we have a concrete example in the next sections on how to use it.

Classes are objects that can live only in a classful qdisc; classes are used in Traffic Control to create hierarchies. Complex hierarchies are made possible by the fact that a class can have filters attached to it, which can then be used as an entry point for another class or for a qdisc.

Classless qdiscs

A classless qdiscs is a qdisc that can't have any children because it is not allowed to have any classes associated. This means that is not possible to attach filters to classless qdiscs. Because classless qdiscs can't have children, we can't add filters and classifiers to them, so classless qdiscs are not interesting from a BPF point of view but still useful for simple Traffic Control needs.

After building up some knowledge on qdiscs, filters, and classes, we now show you how to write BPF programs for a cls_bpf classifier.

Traffic Control Classifier Program Using cls_bpf

As we said, Traffic Control is a powerful mechanism that is made even more powerful thanks to classifiers; however, among all the classifiers, there is one that allows you to program the network data path cls_bpf classifier. This classifier is special because it can run BPF programs, but what does that mean? It means that cls_bpf will allow you to hook your BPF programs directly in the ingress and egress layers, and running BPF programs hooked to those layers means that they will be able to access the sk_buff struct for the respective packets.

To understand better this relationship between Traffic Control and BPF programs, see Figure 6-3, which shows how BPF programs are loaded against the `cls_bpf` classifier. You will also notice that such programs are hooked into ingress and egress qdiscs. All the other interactions in context are also described. By taking the network interface as the entry point for network traffic, you will see the following:

- The traffic first goes to the Traffic Control's ingress hook.
- Then the kernel will execute the BFP program loaded into the ingress from user-space for every request coming in.
- After the ingress program is executed, the control is given to the networking stack that informs the user's application about the networking event.
- After the application gives a response, the control is passed to the Traffic Control's egress using another BPF program that executes, and upon completion gives back control to the kernel.
- A response is given to the client.

You can write BPF programs for Traffic Control in C and compile them using LLVM/ Clang with the BPF backend.

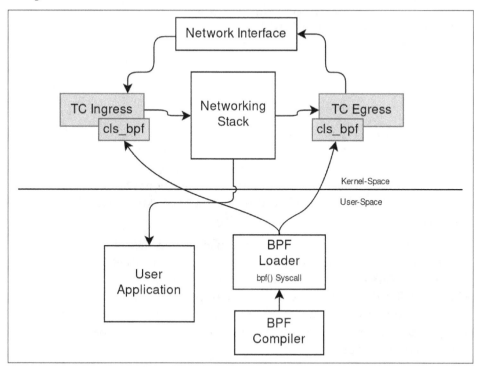

Figure 6-3. Loading of BPF programs using Traffic Control

Ingress and egress qdiscs allow you to hook Traffic Control into inbound (ingress) and outbound (egress) traffic, respectively.

To make this example work, you need to run it on a kernel that has been compiled with cls_bpf directly or as a module. To verify that you have everything you need, you can do the following:

```
cat /proc/config.gz| zcat  | grep -i BPF
```

Make sure you get at least the following output with either y or m:

```
CONFIG_BPF=y
CONFIG_BPF_SYSCALL=y
CONFIG_NET_CLS_BPF=m
CONFIG_BPF_JIT=y
CONFIG_HAVE_EBPF_JIT=y
CONFIG_BPF_EVENTS=y
```

Let's now see how we write the classifier:

```
SEC("classifier")
static inline int classification(struct __sk_buff *skb) {
  void *data_end = (void *)(long)skb->data_end;
  void *data = (void *)(long)skb->data;
  struct ethhdr *eth = data;

  __u16 h_proto;
  __u64 nh_off = 0;
  nh_off = sizeof(*eth);

  if (data + nh_off > data_end) {
    return TC_ACT_OK;
  }
```

The "main" of our classifier is the classification function. This function is annotated with a section header called classifier so that tc can know that this is the classifier to use.

At this point, we need to extract some information from the skb; the data member contains all the data for the current packet and all its protocol details. To let our program know what's inside of it, we need to cast it to an Ethernet frame (in our case, with the *eth variable). To make the static verifier happy, we need to check that the data, summed up with the size of the eth pointer, does not exceed the space where data_end is. After that, we can go one level inward and get the protocol type from the h_proto member in *eth:

```
if (h_proto == bpf_htons(ETH_P_IP)) {
  if (is_http(skb, nh_off) == 1) {
```

```
        trace_printk("Yes! It is HTTP!\n");
    }
}

return TC_ACT_OK;
}
```

After we have the protocol, we need to convert it from the host to check whether it is equal to the IPv4 protocol, the one we are interested in, and if it is, we check whether the inner packet is HTTP using our own is_http function. If it is, we print a debug message stating that we found an HTTP packet:

```
void *data_end = (void *)(long)skb->data_end;
void *data = (void *)(long)skb->data;
struct iphdr *iph = data + nh_off;

if (iph + 1 > data_end) {
  return 0;
}

if (iph->protocol != IPPROTO_TCP) {
  return 0;
}
__u32 tcp_hlen = 0;
```

The is_http function is similar to our classifier function, but it will start from an skb by knowing already the start offset for the IPv4 protocol data. As we did earlier, we need to do a check before accessing the IP protocol data with the *iph variable to let the static verifier know our intentions.

When that's done, we just check whether the IPv4 header contains a TCP packet so that we can go ahead. If the packet's protocol is of type IPPROTO_TCP, we need to do some more checks again to get the actual TCP header in the *tcph variable:

```
plength = ip_total_length - ip_hlen - tcp_hlen;
if (plength >= 7) {
  unsigned long p[7];
  int i = 0;
  for (i = 0; i < 7; i++) {

    p[i] = load_byte(skb, poffset + i);
  }
  int *value;
  if ((p[0] == 'H') && (p[1] == 'T') && (p[2] == 'T') && (p[3] == 'P')) {
    return 1;
  }
}

return 0;
}
```

Now that the TCP header is ours, we can go ahead and load the first seven bytes from the skb struct at the offset of the TCP payload poffset. At this point we can check whether the bytes array is a sequence saying HTTP; then we know that the Layer 7 protocol is HTTP, and we can return 1—otherwise, we return zero.

As you can see, our program is simple. It will basically allow everything, and when receiving an HTTP packet, it will let us know with a debugging message.

You can compile the program with Clang, using the bpf target, as we did before with the socket filter example. We cannot compile this program for Traffic Control in the same way; this will generate an *ELF* file classifier.o that will be loaded by tc this time and not by our own custom loader:

```
clang -O2 -target bpf -c classifier.c -o classifier.o
```

Traffic Control Return Codes

From man 8 tc-bpf:

TC_ACT_OK (0)
: Terminates the packet processing pipeline and allows the packet to proceed

TC_ACT_SHOT (2)
: Terminates the packet processing pipeline and drops the packet

TC_ACT_UNSPEC (-1)
: Uses the default action configured from tc (similarly as returning –1 from a classifier)

TC_ACT_PIPE (3)
: Iterates to the next action, if available

TC_ACT_RECLASSIFY (1)
: Terminates the packet processing pipeline and starts classification from the beginning else

Everything else is an unspecified return code

Now we can install the program on the interface we want our program to operate on; in our case, it was eth0.

The first command will replace the default qdisc for the eth0 device, and the second one will actually load our cls_bpf classifier into that ingress classful qdisc. This means that our program will handle all traffic going into that interface. If we want to handle outgoing traffic, we would need to use the egress qdisc instead:

```
# tc qdisc add dev eth0 handle 0: ingress
# tc filter add dev eth0 ingress bpf obj classifier.o flowid 0:
```

Our program is loaded now—what we need is to send some HTTP traffic to that interface.

To do that you need any HTTP server on that interface. Then you can `curl` the interface IP.

In case you don't have one, you can obtain a test HTTP server using Python 3 with the `http.server` module. It will open the port 8000 with a directory listing of the current working directory:

```
python3 -m http.server
```

At this point you can call the server with `curl`:

```
$ curl http://192.168.1.63:8080
```

After doing that you should see your HTTP response from the HTTP server. You can now get your debugging messages (created with `trace_printk`), confirming that using the dedicated `tc` command:

```
# tc exec bpf dbg
```

The output will be something like this:

```
Running! Hang up with ^C!

        python3-18456 [000] ..s1 283544.114997: 0: Yes! It is HTTP!
        python3-18754 [002] ..s1 283566.008163: 0: Yes! It is HTTP!
```

Congratulations! You just made your first BPF Traffic Control classifier.

 Instead of using a debugging message like we did in this example, you could use a map to communicate to user-space that the interface just received an HTTP packet. We leave this as an exercise for you to do. If you look at `classifier.c` in the previous example, you can get an idea of how to do that by looking at how we used the map `countmap` there.

At this point, what you might want is to unload the classifier. You can do that by deleting the ingress qdisc that you just attached to the interface:

```
# tc qdisc del dev eth0 ingress
```

Notes on act_bpf and how cls_bpf is different

You might have noticed that another object exists for BPF programs called `act_bpf`. It turns out that `act_bpf` is an action, not a classifier. This makes it operationally different because actions are objects attached to filters, and because of this it is not able to perform filtering directly, requiring Traffic Control to consider all the packets first. For this property, it is usually preferable to use the `cls_bpf` classifier instead of the `act_bpf` action.

However, because `act_bpf` can be attached to any classifier, there might be cases for which you find it useful to just reuse a classifier you already have and attach a BPF program to it.

Differences Between Traffic Control and XDP

Even though the Traffic Control `cls_bpf` and XDP programs look very similar, they are pretty different. XDP programs are executed earlier in the ingress data path, before entering into the main kernel network stack, so our program does not have access to a socket buffer struct `sk_buff` like with `tc`. XDP programs instead take a different structure called `xdp_buff`, which is an eager representation of the packet without metadata. All this comes with advantages and disadvantages. For example, being executed even before the kernel code, XDP programs can drop packets in an efficient way. Compared to Traffic Control programs, XDP programs can be attached only to traffic in ingress to the system.

At this point, you might be asking yourself when it's an advantage to use one instead of the other. The answer is that because of their nature of not containing all the kernel-enriched data structures and metadata, XDP programs are better for use cases covering OSI layers up to Layer 4. But let's not spoil all the content of the next chapter!

Conclusion

It should now be pretty clear to you that BPF programs are useful for getting visibility and control at different levels of the networking data path. You've seen how to take advantage of them to filter packets using high-level tools that generate a BPF assembly. Then we loaded a program to a network socket, and in the end we attached our programs to the Traffic Control ingress qdisc to do traffic classification using BPF programs. In this chapter we also briefly discussed XDP, but be prepared, because in Chapter 7 we cover the topic in its entirety by expanding on how XDP programs are constructed, what kind of XDP programs there are, and how to write and test them.

Express Data Path

Express Data Path (XDP) is a safe, programmable, high-performance, kernel-integrated packet processor in the Linux network data path that executes BPF programs when the NIC driver receives a packet. This allows XDP programs to make decisions regarding the received packet (drop, modify, or just allow it) at the earliest possible point in time.

The execution point is not the only aspect that makes XDP programs fast; other design decisions play a role in that:

- There are no memory allocations while doing packet processing with XDP.
- XDP programs work only with linear, unfragmented packets and have the start and end pointers of the packet.
- There's no access to full packet metadata, which is why the input context this kind of program receives will be of type xdp_buff instead of the sk_buff struct you encountered in Chapter 6.
- Because they are eBPF programs, XDP programs have a bounded execution time, and the consequence of this is that their usage has a fixed cost in the networking pipeline.

When talking about XDP, it is important to remember that it is not a kernel bypass mechanism; it is designed to be integrated with other kernel components and the internal Linux security model.

The `xdp_buff` struct is used to present a packet context to a BPF program that uses the direct packet access mechanism provided by the XDP framework. Think of it as a "lightweight" version of the `sk_buff`.

The difference between the two is that `sk_buff` also holds and allows you to mingle with the packets' metadata (proto, mark, type), which is only available at a higher level in the networking pipeline. The fact that `xdp_buff` is created early and doesn't depend on other kernel layers is one reason it's faster to obtain and process packets using XDP. The other reason is that `xdp_buff` doesn't hold references to routes, Traffic Control hooks, or other kind of packet metadata like it would with program types that use an `sk_buff`.

In this chapter we explore the characteristics of XDP programs, the different kinds of XDP programs out there, and how they can be compiled and loaded. After that, to give more context, we discuss real-world use cases for it.

XDP Programs Overview

Essentially, what XDP programs do is that they make determinations about the received packet, and then they can edit the received packet's content or just return a result code. The result code is used to determine what happens to the packet in the form of an action. You can drop the packet, you can transmit it out the same interface, or you can pass it up to the rest of the networking stack. Additionally, to cooperate with the network stack, XDP programs can push and pull a packet's headers; for example, if the current kernel does not support an encapsulation format or a protocol, an XDP program can de-encapsulate it or translate the protocol and send the result to the kernel for processing.

But wait, what's the correlation between XDP and eBPF?

It turns out that XDP programs are controlled through the `bpf` syscall and loaded using the program type `BPF_PROG_TYPE_XDP`. Also, the execution driver hook executes BPF bytecode.

An important concept to understand when writing XDP programs is that the contexts where they will run are also called *operation modes*.

Operation Modes

XDP has three operation modes to accommodate easily testing functions, custom hardware from vendors, and commonly built kernels without custom hardware. Let's go over each of them.

Native XDP

This is the default mode. In this mode, the XDP BPF program is run directly out of the networking driver's early receive path. When using this mode, it's important to check whether the driver supports it. You can check that by executing the following command against the source tree of a given kernel version:

```
# Clone the linux-stable repository
git clone git://git.kernel.org/pub/scm/linux/kernel/git/stable/linux-stable.git\
linux-stable

# Checkout the tag for your current kernel version
cd linux-stable
git checkout tags/v4.18

# Check the available drivers
git grep -l XDP_SETUP_PROG drivers/
```

That produces output like this:

```
drivers/net/ethernet/broadcom/bnxt/bnxt_xdp.c
drivers/net/ethernet/cavium/thunder/nicvf_main.c
drivers/net/ethernet/intel/i40e/i40e_main.c
drivers/net/ethernet/intel/ixgbe/ixgbe_main.c
drivers/net/ethernet/intel/ixgbevf/ixgbevf_main.c
drivers/net/ethernet/mellanox/mlx4/en_netdev.c
drivers/net/ethernet/mellanox/mlx5/core/en_main.c
drivers/net/ethernet/netronome/nfp/nfp_net_common.c
drivers/net/ethernet/qlogic/qede/qede_filter.c
drivers/net/netdevsim/bpf.c
drivers/net/tun.c
drivers/net/virtio_net.c
```

From what we can see, kernel 4.18 supports the following:

- Broadcom NetXtreme-C/E network driver bnxt
- Cavium thunderx driver
- Intel i40 driver
- Intel ixgbe and ixgvevf drivers
- Mellanox mlx4 and mlx5 drivers
- Netronome Network Flow Processor
- QLogic qede NIC Driver
- TUN/TAP
- Virtio

With a clear idea of the native operation mode, we can proceed to see how XDP program duties can be directly handled by network cards by using offloaded XDP.

Offloaded XDP

In this mode the XDP BPF program is directly offloaded into the NIC instead of being executed on the host CPU. By pushing execution off of the CPU, this mode has high-performance gains over native XDP.

We can reuse the kernel source tree we just cloned to check what NIC drivers in 4.18 support hardware offload by looking for XDP_SETUP_PROG_HW:

```
git grep -l XDP_SETUP_PROG_HW drivers/
```

That should output something like this:

```
include/linux/netdevice.h
866:    XDP_SETUP_PROG_HW,

net/core/dev.c
8001:           xdp.command = XDP_SETUP_PROG_HW;

drivers/net/netdevsim/bpf.c
200:    if (bpf->command == XDP_SETUP_PROG_HW && !ns->bpf_xdpoffload_accept) {
205:    if (bpf->command == XDP_SETUP_PROG_HW) {
560:    case XDP_SETUP_PROG_HW:

drivers/net/ethernet/netronome/nfp/nfp_net_common.c
3476:   case XDP_SETUP_PROG_HW:
```

That shows only the Netronome Network Flow Processor (nfp) meaning that it can operate in both modes by also supporting hardware offload along with native XDP.

Now a good question for yourself might be, what do I do when I don't have network cards and drivers to try my XDP programs? The answer is easy, generic XDP!

Generic XDP

This is provided as a test-mode for developers who want to write and run XDP programs without having the capabilities of native or offloaded XDP. Generic XDP has been supported since kernel version 4.12. You can use this mode, for example, on veth devices—we use this mode in the subsequent examples to show the capabilities of XDP without requiring you to buy specific hardware to follow along.

But who is the actor responsible for the coordination between all of the components and the operation modes? Continue to the next section to learn about the packet processor.

The Packet Processor

The actor that makes it possible to execute BPF programs on XDP packets and that coordinates the interaction between them and the network stack is the XDP packet processor. The packet processor is the in-kernel component for XDP programs that processes packets on the receive (RX) queue directly as they are presented by the NIC. It ensures that packets are readable and writable and allows you to attach post-processing verdicts in the form of packet processor actions. Atomic program updates and new program loads to the packet processor can be done at runtime without any service interruption in terms of networking and associated traffic. While operating, XDP can be used in "busy polling" mode, allowing you to reserve the CPUs that will have to deal with each RX queue; this avoids context switches and allows immediate packet reactivity upon arrival regardless of IRQ affinities. The other mode XDP can be used in is the "interrupt driven" mode that, on the other hand, does not reserve the CPU but instructs an interrupt acting as an event medium to inform the CPU that it has to deal with a new event while still doing normal processing.

In Figure 7-1 you can see in the interaction points between RX/TX, applications, the packet processor, and the BPF programs applied to its packets.

Notice that there are a few squares with a string prepended by XDP_ in Figure 7-1. Those are the XDP result codes, which we cover next.

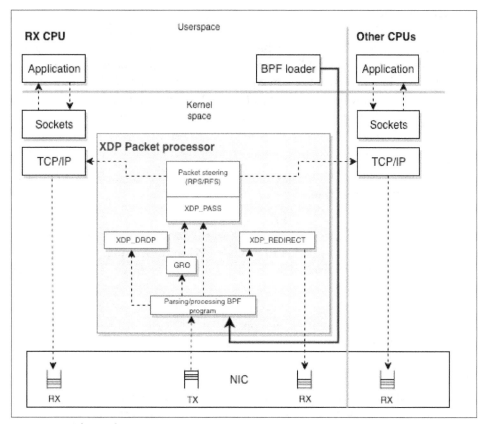

Figure 7-1. The packet processor

XDP result codes (packet processor actions)

After a decision is made about the packet in the packet processor, it can be expressed using one of the five return codes that then can instruct the network driver on how to process the packet. Let's dive into the actions that the packet processor performs:

Drop (XDP_DROP)
> Drops the packet. This happens at the earliest RX stage in the driver; dropping a packet simply implies recycling it back into the RX ring queue it just "arrived" on. Dropping the packet as early as possible is key for the denial-of-service (DoS) mitigation use cases. This way, dropped packets use as little CPU processing time and power as possible.

Forward (XDP_TX)
> Forwards the packet. This can happen before or after the packet has been modified. Forwarding a packet implies bouncing the received packet page back out the same NIC it arrived on.

Redirect (XDP_REDIRECT)
> Similar to XDP_TX in that it is able to transmit the XDP packet, but it does so through another NIC or into a BPF cpumap. In the case of a BPF cpumap, the CPUs serving XDP on the NIC's receive queues can continue to do so and push the packet for processing the upper kernel stack to a remote CPU. This is similar to XDP_PASS, but with the ability that the XDP BPF program can keep serving the incoming high load as opposed to temporarily spending work on the current packet for pushing into the upper layers.

Pass (XDP_PASS)
> Passes the packet to the normal network stack for processing. This is equivalent to the default packet handling behavior without XDP. This can be done in one of two ways:
>
> - *Normal receive* allocates metadata (sk_buff), receives the packet onto the stack, and steers the packet to another CPU for processing. It allows for raw interfaces to user-space. This can happen before or after the packet has been modified.
>
> - *Generic receive offload* (GRO) can perform a receive of large packets and combines packets of the same connection. GRO eventually passes the packet through the "normal receive" flow after processing.

Code error (XDP_ABORTED)
> Denotes an eBPF program error and results in the packet being dropped. It is not something a functional program should ever use as a return code. For example, XDP_ABORTED would be returned if the program divided by zero. XDP_ABORTED's

value will always be zero. It passes the `trace_xdp_exception` tracepoint, which can be additionally monitored to detect misbehavior.

These action codes are expressed in the `linux/bpf.h` header file as follows:

```
enum xdp_action {
    XDP_ABORTED = 0,
    XDP_DROP,
    XDP_PASS,
    XDP_TX,
    XDP_REDIRECT,
};
```

Because XDP actions determine different behaviors and are an internal mechanism of the packet processor, you can look at a simplified version of Figure 7-1 focused on only the return actions (see Figure 7-2).

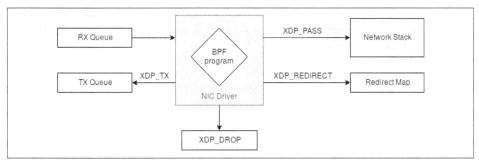

Figure 7-2. XDP action codes

An interesting thing about XDP programs is that you don't usually need to write a loader to load them. There is a good loader in most Linux machines implemented by the `ip` command. The next section describes how to use it.

XDP and iproute2 as a Loader

The `ip` command, available in iproute2 (*https://oreil.ly/65zuT*), has the ability to act as a frontend to load XDP programs compiled into an ELF file and has full support for maps, map relocation, tail call and object pinning.

Because loading an XDP program can be expressed as a configuration of an existing network interface, the loader is implemented as part of the `ip link` command, which is the one that does network device configuration.

The syntax to load the XDP program is simple:

```
# ip link set dev eth0 xdp obj program.o sec mysection
```

Let's analyze this command parameter by parameter:

ip
> This invokes the `ip` command.

link
> Configures network interfaces.

set
> Changes device attributes.

dev eth0
> Specifies the network device on which we want to operate and load the XDP program.

xdp obj program.o
> Loads an XDP program from the ELF file (object) named `program.o`. The `xdp` part of this command tells the system to use the native driver when it is available and fallback to generic otherwise. You can force using a mode or another by using a more specific selector:
>
> - xdpgeneric to use generic XDP
>
> - xdpdrv to use native XDP
>
> - xdpoffload to use offloaded XDP

sec mysection
> Specifies the section name `mysection` containing the BPF program to use from the ELF file; if this is not specified, the section named `prog` will be used. If no section is specified in the program, you have to specify `sec .text` in the `ip` invocation.

Let's see a practical example.

The scenario is that we have a system with a web server on port 8000 for which we want to block any access to its pages on the public-facing NIC of the server by disallowing all the TCP connections to it.

The first thing that we will need is the web server in question; if you don't already have one, you can start one with `python3`.

```
$ python3 -m http.server
```

After your webserver is started, its open port will be shown in the open sockets using `ss`. As you can see the webserver is bound to any interface, `*:8000`, so as of now, any external caller with access to our public interfaces will be able to see its content!

```
$ ss -tulpn
Netid  State      Recv-Q Send-Q Local Address:Port   Peer Address:Port
tcp    LISTEN     0      5      *:8000               *:*
```

Socket statistics, `ss` in the terminal, is a command-line utility used to investigate network sockets in Linux. It is effectively a modern version of `netstat`, and its user experience is similar to Netstat, meaning that you can pass the same arguments and get comparable results.

At this point, we can inspect the network interfaces on the machine that's running our HTTP server:

```
$ ip a
1: lo: <LOOPBACK,UP,LOWER_UP> mtu 65536 qdisc noqueue state UNKNOWN group defau
lt qlen 1000
    link/loopback 00:00:00:00:00:00 brd 00:00:00:00:00:00
    inet 127.0.0.1/8 scope host lo
       valid_lft forever preferred_lft forever
    inet6 ::1/128 scope host
       valid_lft forever preferred_lft forever
2: enp0s3: <BROADCAST,MULTICAST,UP,LOWER_UP> mtu 1500 qdisc fq_codel state UP g
roup default qlen 1000
    link/ether 02:1e:30:9c:a3:c0 brd ff:ff:ff:ff:ff:ff
    inet 10.0.2.15/24 brd 10.0.2.255 scope global dynamic enp0s3
       valid_lft 84964sec preferred_lft 84964sec
    inet6 fe80::1e:30ff:fe9c:a3c0/64 scope link
       valid_lft forever preferred_lft forever
3: enp0s8: <BROADCAST,MULTICAST,UP,LOWER_UP> mtu 1500 qdisc fq_codel state UP g
roup default qlen 1000
    link/ether 08:00:27:0d:15:7d brd ff:ff:ff:ff:ff:ff
    inet 192.168.33.11/24 brd 192.168.33.255 scope global enp0s8
       valid_lft forever preferred_lft forever
    inet6 fe80::a00:27ff:fe0d:157d/64 scope link
       valid_lft forever preferred_lft forever
```

Notice that this machine has three interfaces, and the network topology is simple:

lo

This is just the loopback interface for internal communication.

enp0s3

This is the management network tier; administrators will use this interface to connect to the web server to do their operations.

enp0s8

This is the interface open to the public, our web server will need to be hidden from this interface.

Now, before loading any XDP program, we can check open ports on the server from another server that can access its network interface, in our case, with IPv4 `192.168.33.11`.

You can check open ports on a remote host by using `nmap` as follows:

```
# nmap -sS 192.168.33.11
Starting Nmap 7.70 ( https://nmap.org ) at 2019-04-06 23:57 CEST
Nmap scan report for 192.168.33.11
Host is up (0.0034s latency).
Not shown: 998 closed ports
PORT     STATE SERVICE
22/tcp   open  ssh
8000/tcp open  http-alt
```

Good! Port 8000 is right there, at this point we need to block it!

 Network Mapper (nmap) is a network scanner that can do host, service, network, and port discovery along with operating system detection. Its main use cases are security auditing and network scanning. When scanning a host for open ports, nmap will try every port in the specified (or full) range.

Our program will consist of a single source file named *program.c*, so let's see what we need to write.

It needs to use the IPv4 iphdr and Ethernet Frame ethhdr header structs and also protocol constants and other structs. Let's include the needed headers, as shown here:

```
#include <linux/bpf.h>
#include <linux/if_ether.h>
#include <linux/in.h>
#include <linux/ip.h>
```

After the headers are included, we can declare the SEC macro we already met in the previous chapters, used to declare ELF attributes.

```
#define SEC(NAME) __attribute__((section(NAME), used))
```

Now we can declare the main entry point for our program, myprogram, and its ELF section name, mysection. Our program takes as input context an xdp_md struct pointer, the BPF equivalent of the in-driver xdp_buff. By using that as the context, we then define the variables we will use next such as the data pointers, the Ethernet, and IP layer structs:

```
SEC("mysection")
int myprogram(struct xdp_md *ctx) {
  int ipsize = 0;
  void *data = (void *)(long)ctx->data;
  void *data_end = (void *)(long)ctx->data_end;
  struct ethhdr *eth = data;
  struct iphdr *ip;
```

Because data contains the Ethernet frame, we can now extract the IPv4 layer from it. We also check that the offset where we look for the IPv4 layer doesn't exceed the

---

whole pointer space so that the static verifier stays happy. When the address space is exceeded we just drop the packet:

```
ipsize = sizeof(*eth);
ip = data + ipsize;
ipsize += sizeof(struct iphdr);
if (data + ipsize > data_end) {
  return XDP_DROP;
}
```

Now, after all the verifications and setup, we can implement the real logic for the program, which basically drops every TCP packet while allowing anything else:

```
if (ip->protocol == IPPROTO_TCP) {
  return XDP_DROP;
}

return XDP_PASS;
}
```

Now that our program is done, we can save it as *program.c.*

The next step is to compile the ELF file *program.o* out of our program using Clang. We can do this compilation step outside the target machine because BPF ELF binaries are not platform dependent:

```
$ clang -O2 -target bpf -c program.c -o program.o
```

Now back on the machine hosting our web server, we can finally load `program.o` against the public network interface `enp0s8` using the `ip` utility with the `set` command, as described earlier:

```
# ip link set dev enp0s8 xdp obj program.o sec mysection
```

As you might notice, we select the section `mysection` as the entry point for the program.

At this stage, if that command returned zero as the exit code with no errors, we can check the network interface to see whether the program had been loaded correctly:

```
# ip a show enp0s8
3: enp0s8: <BROADCAST,MULTICAST,UP,LOWER_UP> mtu 1500 xdpgeneric/id:32
    qdisc fq_codel state UP group default qlen 1000
    link/ether 08:00:27:0d:15:7d brd ff:ff:ff:ff:ff:ff
    inet 192.168.33.11/24 brd 192.168.33.255 scope global enp0s8
       valid_lft forever preferred_lft forever
    inet6 fe80::a00:27ff:fe0d:157d/64 scope link
       valid_lft forever preferred_lft forever
```

As you can see, our output for `ip a` now has a new detail; after the MTU, it shows `xdpgeneric/id:32`, which is showing two interesting bits of information:

- The driver that had been used, `xdpgeneric`

- The ID of the XDP program, 32

The last step is to verify that the loaded program is in fact doing what it is supposed to do. We can verify that by executing `nmap` again on an external machine to observe that port 8000 is no longer reachable:

```
# nmap -sS 192.168.33.11
Starting Nmap 7.70 ( https://nmap.org ) at 2019-04-07 01:07 CEST
Nmap scan report for 192.168.33.11
Host is up (0.00039s latency).
Not shown: 998 closed ports
PORT    STATE SERVICE
22/tcp  open  ssh
```

Another test to verify that it all works can be trying to access the program through a browser or doing any HTTP request. Any kind of test should fail when targeting `192.168.33.11` as the destination. Good job and congratulations on loading your first XDP program!

If you followed all of those steps on a machine that you need to restore to its original state, you can always detach the program and turn off XDP for the device:

```
# ip link set dev enp0s8 xdp off
```

Interesting! Loading XDP programs seems easy, doesn't it?

At least when using `iproute2` as the loader, you can skip the part of having to write a loader yourself. In this example, our focus was on `iproute2`, which already implements a loader for XDP programs. However, the programs are in fact BPF programs, so even if `iproute2` can be handy sometimes, you should always remember that you can load your programs using BCC, as shown in the next section, or you can use the bpf syscall directly. Having a custom loader has the advantage of allowing you to manage the lifecycle of the program and its interactions with user-space.

XDP and BCC

Like with any other BPF program, XDP programs can be compiled, loaded, and run using BCC. The following example shows an XDP program that is similar to the one we used for `iproute2` but that has a custom user-space loader made with BCC. The loader in this case is needed because we also want to count the number of packets we encounter while dropping TCP packets.

Like before, we create a kernel-space program named *program.c* first.

In the `iproute2` example, our program needed to import the required headers for struct and function definitions related to BPF and protocols. Here we do the same, but we also declare a map of type `BPF_MAP_TYPE_PERCPU_ARRAY` using the `BPF_TABLE` macro. The map will contain a packet counter for each IP protocol index, which is the reason for the size 256 (the IP specification contains only 256 values). We want to use a `BPF_MAP_TYPE_PERCPU_ARRAY` type because that's the one that guarantees atomicity of the counters at CPU level without locking:

```
#define KBUILD_MODNAME "program"
#include <linux/bpf.h>
#include <linux/in.h>
#include <linux/ip.h>

BPF_TABLE("percpu_array", uint32_t, long, packetcnt, 256);
```

After that, we declare our main function, `myprogram`, which takes as a parameter the `xdp_md` struct. The first thing this needs to contain is the variable declarations for the Ethernet IPv4 frames:

```
int myprogram(struct xdp_md *ctx) {
  int ipsize = 0;
  void *data = (void *)(long)ctx->data;
  void *data_end = (void *)(long)ctx->data_end;
  struct ethhdr *eth = data;
  struct iphdr *ip;
  long *cnt;
  __u32 idx;

  ipsize = sizeof(*eth);
  ip = data + ipsize;
  ipsize += sizeof(struct iphdr);
```

After we have all the variable declarations done and can access the `data` pointer that now contains the Ethernet frame and the `ip` pointer with the IPv4 packet, we can check whether the memory space is out of bounds. If it is, we drop the packet. If the memory space is OK, we extract the protocol and lookup the `packetcnt` array to get the previous value of the packet counter for the current protocol in the variable `idx`. Then we increment the counter by one. When the increment is handled, we can proceed and check whether the protocol is TCP. If it is, we just drop the packet without questioning; otherwise, we allow it:

```
  if (data + ipsize > data_end) {
    return XDP_DROP;
  }

  idx = ip->protocol;
  cnt = packetcnt.lookup(&idx);
  if (cnt) {
    *cnt += 1;
  }

  if (ip->protocol == IPPROTO_TCP) {
    return XDP_DROP;
  }
```

```
        return XDP_PASS;
    }
```

Now let's write the loader: loader.py.

It is made of two parts: the actual loading logic and the loop that prints the packet counts.

For the loading logic, we open our program by reading the file *program.c.* With load_func, we instruct the bpf syscall to use the myprogram function as "main" using the program type BPF.XDP. That stands for BPF_PROG_TYPE_XDP.

After the loading, we gain access to the BPF map named packetcnt using get_table.

 Make sure to change the device variable from enp0s8 to the interface you want to work on.

```
#!/usr/bin/python

from bcc import BPF
import time
import sys

device = "enp0s8"
b = BPF(src_file="program.c")
fn = b.load_func("myprogram", BPF.XDP)
b.attach_xdp(device, fn, 0)
packetcnt = b.get_table("packetcnt")
```

The remaining part we need to write is the actual loop to print out the packet counts. Without this, our program will already be able to drop the packets, but we want to see what's going on there. We have two loops. The outer loop gets keyboard events and terminates when there's a signal to interrupt the program. When the outer loop breaks, the remove_xdp function is called, and the interface is freed from the XDP program.

Within the outer loop, the inner loop has the duty of getting back the values from the packetcnt map and prints them in the format *protocol: counter* pkt/s:

```
prev = [0] * 256
print("Printing packet counts per IP protocol-number, hit CTRL+C to stop")
while 1:
    try:
        for k in packetcnt.keys():
            val = packetcnt.sum(k).value
            i = k.value
            if val:
```

```
                delta = val - prev[i]
                prev[i] = val
                print("{}: {} pkt/s".format(i, delta))
            time.sleep(1)
        except KeyboardInterrupt:
            print("Removing filter from device")
            break

    b.remove_xdp(device, 0)
```

Good! Now we can test that program by simply executing the loader with root privileges:

```
# python program.py
```

That will output a line every second with the packet counters:

```
Printing packet counts per IP protocol-number, hit CTRL+C to stop
6: 10 pkt/s
17: 3 pkt/s
^CRemoving filter from device
```

We encountered only two types of packets: 6 stands for TCP, and 17 stands for UDP.

At this point your brain will probably start thinking about ideas and projects for using XDP, and that's extremely good! But as always, in software engineering if you want to make a good program, it's important to write tests first—or at least write tests! The next section covers how you can unit-test XDP programs.

Testing XDP Programs

When working on XDP programs, the most difficult part is that in order to test the actual packet flow, you need to reproduce an environment in which all of the components are aligned to provide the correct packets. Although it's true that with virtualization technologies nowadays, creating a working environment can be an easy task, it's also true that a complicated setup can limit the reproducibility and programmability of the test environment. In addition to that, when analyzing the performance aspects of high-frequency XDP programs in a virtualized environment, the cost of virtualization makes the test ineffective because it's much more substantial than the actual packet processing.

Fortunately, kernel developers have a solution. They have implemented a command that can be used to test XDP programs, called BPF_PROG_TEST_RUN.

Essentially, BPF_PROG_TEST_RUN gets an XDP program to execute, along with an input packet and an output packet. When the program is executed, the output packet variable is populated, and the return XDP code is returned. This means you can use the output packet and return code in your test assertions! This technique can also be used for skb programs.

For the sake of completeness and to make this example simple, we use Python and its unit testing framework.

XDP Testing Using the Python Unit Testing Framework

Writing XDP tests with `BPF_PROG_TEST_RUN` and integrating them with the Python unit testing framework `unittest` is a good idea for several reasons:

- You can load and execute BPF programs using the Python *BCC* library.
- Python has one of the best packet crafting and introspection libraries available: `scapy`.
- Python integrates with C structs using `ctypes`.

As said, we need to import all of the needed libraries; that's the first thing we will do in a file named *test_xdp.py*:

```
from bcc import BPF, libbcc
from scapy.all import Ether, IP, raw, TCP, UDP

import ctypes
import unittest


class XDPExampleTestCase(unittest.TestCase):
    SKB_OUT_SIZE = 1514  # mtu 1500 + 14 ethernet size
    bpf_function = None
```

After all the needed libraries are imported, we can proceed and create a test case class named `XDPExampleTestCase`. This test class will contain all of our test cases and a member method (`_xdp_test_run`) that we will use to do assertions and call `bpf_prog_test_run`.

In the following code you can see what `_xdp_test_run` looks like:

```
    def _xdp_test_run(self, given_packet, expected_packet, expected_return):
        size = len(given_packet)

        given_packet = ctypes.create_string_buffer(raw(given_packet), size)
        packet_output = ctypes.create_string_buffer(self.SKB_OUT_SIZE)

        packet_output_size = ctypes.c_uint32()
        test_retval = ctypes.c_uint32()
        duration = ctypes.c_uint32()
        repeat = 1
        ret = libbcc.lib.bpf_prog_test_run(self.bpf_function.fd,
                                           repeat,
                                           ctypes.byref(given_packet),
                                           size,
                                           ctypes.byref(packet_output),
```

```
                                        ctypes.byref(packet_output_size),
                                        ctypes.byref(test_retval),
                                        ctypes.byref(duration))
        self.assertEqual(ret, 0)
        self.assertEqual(test_retval.value, expected_return)

        if expected_packet:
            self.assertEqual(
                packet_output[:packet_output_size.value], raw(expected_packet))
```

It takes three arguments:

given_packet

This is the packet we test our XDP program against; it is the raw packet received by the interface.

expected_packet

This is the packet we expect to receive back after the XDP program processes it; when the XDP program returns an XDP_DROP or XDP_ABORT, we expect this to be None; in all the other cases, the packet remains the same as given_packet or can be modified.

expected_return

This is the expected return of the XDP program after processing our given_packet.

Besides the arguments, the body of this method is simple. It does conversion to C types using the *ctypes* library, and then it calls the libbcc equivalent of BPF_PROG_TEST_RUN, libbcc.lib.bpf_prog_test_run, using as test arguments our packets and their metadata. Then it does all of the assertions based on the results from the test call along with the given values.

After we have that function we can basically just write test cases by crafting different packets to test how they behave when passing through our XDP program, but before doing that, we need to do a setUp method for our test.

This part is crucial because the setup does the actual load of our BPF program named myprogram by opening and compiling a source file named *program.c* (that's the file where our XDP code will be):

```
def setUp(self):
    bpf_prog = BPF(src_file=b"program.c")
    self.bpf_function = bpf_prog.load_func(b"myprogram", BPF.XDP)
```

After the setup is done, the next step is to write the first behavior we want to observe. Without being too imaginative, we want to test that we will drop all TCP packets.

So we craft a packet in `given_packet`, which is just a TCP packet over IPv4. Then, using our assertion method, `_xdp_test_run`, we just verify that given our packet, we will get back an `XDP_DROP` with no return packet:

```
def test_drop_tcp(self):
    given_packet = Ether() / IP() / TCP()
    self._xdp_test_run(given_packet, None, BPF.XDP_DROP)
```

Because that is not enough, we also want to explicitly test that all UDP packets are allowed. We then craft two UDP packets, one for `given_packet` and one for `expected_packet`, that are essentially the same. In that way we are also testing that UDP packets are not modified while being allowed with XDP_PASS:

```
def test_pass_udp(self):
    given_packet = Ether() / IP() / UDP()
    expected_packet = Ether() / IP() / UDP()
    self._xdp_test_run(given_packet, expected_packet, BPF.XDP_PASS)
```

To make things a bit more complicated, we decided that this system will then allow TCP packets on the condition that they go to port 9090. When they do, they will also be rewritten to change their destination MAC address to redirect to a specific network interface with address `08:00:27:dd:38:2a`.

Here's the test case to do that. The `given_packet` has `9090` as a destination port, and we require the `expected_packet` with the new destination and port 9090 again:

```
def test_transform_dst(self):
    given_packet = Ether() / IP() / TCP(dport=9090)
    expected_packet = Ether(dst='08:00:27:dd:38:2a') / \
        IP() / TCP(dport=9090)
    self._xdp_test_run(given_packet, expected_packet, BPF.XDP_TX)
```

With plenty of test cases, we now write the entry point for our test program, which will just call `unittest.main()` that then loads and executes our tests:

```
if __name__ == '__main__':
    unittest.main()
```

We have now written tests for our XDP program first! Now that we have the test acting as a specific example of what we want to have, we can write the XDP program that implements it by creating a file named *program.c*.

Our program is simple. It just contains the `myprogram` XDP function with the logic we just tested. As always, the first thing we need to do is to include the needed headers. Those headers are self-explainatory. We have a BPF program that will process TCP/IP flowing over Ethernet:

```
#define KBUILD_MODNAME "kmyprogram"

#include <linux/bpf.h>
#include <linux/if_ether.h>
```

```
#include <linux/tcp.h>
#include <linux/in.h>
#include <linux/ip.h>
```

Again, as with the other programs in this chapter, we need to check offsets and fill variables for the three layers of our packet: ethhdr, iphdr, and tcphdr, respectively, for Ethernet, IPv4, and TCP:

```
int myprogram(struct xdp_md *ctx) {
  int ipsize = 0;
  void *data = (void *)(long)ctx->data;
  void *data_end = (void *)(long)ctx->data_end;
  struct ethhdr *eth = data;
  struct iphdr *ip;
  struct tcphdr *th;

  ipsize = sizeof(*eth);
  ip = data + ipsize;
  ipsize += sizeof(struct iphdr);
  if (data + ipsize > data_end) {
    return XDP_DROP;
  }
```

Once we have the values we can implement our logic.

The first thing we do is to check whether the protocol is TCP ip->protocol == IPPROTO_TCP. When it is, we always do an XDP_DROP; otherwise, we do an XDP_PASS for everything else.

In the check for the TCP protocol, we do another control to check whether the destination port is 9090, th->dest == htons(9090); if it is, we change the destination MAC address at the Ethernet layer and return XDP_TX to bounce the packet through the same NIC:

```
  if (ip->protocol == IPPROTO_TCP) {
    th = (struct tcphdr *)(ip + 1);
    if ((void *)(th + 1) > data_end) {
      return XDP_DROP;
    }

    if (th->dest == htons(9090)) {
      eth->h_dest[0] = 0x08;
      eth->h_dest[1] = 0x00;
      eth->h_dest[2] = 0x27;
      eth->h_dest[3] = 0xdd;
      eth->h_dest[4] = 0x38;
      eth->h_dest[5] = 0x2a;
      return XDP_TX;
    }

    return XDP_DROP;
  }
```

```
    return XDP_PASS;
  }
```

Amazing! Now we can just run our tests:

```
sudo python test_xdp.py
```

The output of it will just report that the three tests passed:

```
...
------------------------------
Ran 3 tests in 4.676s

OK
```

At this point, breaking things is easier! We can just change the last XDP_PASS to XDP_DROP in *program.c* and observe what happens:

```
.F.
======================================================================
FAIL: test_pass_udp (__main__.XDPExampleTestCase)
----------------------------------------------------------------------
Traceback (most recent call last):
  File "test_xdp.py", line 48, in test_pass_udp
    self._xdp_test_run(given_packet, expected_packet, BPF.XDP_PASS)
  File "test_xdp.py", line 31, in _xdp_test_run
    self.assertEqual(test_retval.value, expected_return)
AssertionError: 1 != 2

----------------------------------------------------------------------
Ran 3 tests in 4.667s

FAILED (failures=1)
```

Our test failed—the status code did not match, and the test framework reported an error. That's exactly what we wanted! This is an effective testing framework to write XDP programs with confidence. We now have the ability to make assertions on specific steps and change them accordingly to the behavior that we want to obtain. Then we write the matching code to express that behavior in the form of an XDP program.

 MAC address is short for Media Access Controll address. It is a unique identifier made of two groups of hexadecimal digits that every network interface has and is used in the data link layer (layer 2 in the OSI model) to interconnect devices over technologies like Ethernet, Bluetooth, and WiFi.

XDP Use Cases

While approaching XDP, it is certainly useful to understand the use cases for which it has been employed by various organizations around the globe. This can help you to imagine why using XDP is better than other techniques such as socket filtering or Traffic Control in certain cases.

Let's begin with a common one: monitoring.

Monitoring

Nowadays, most of the network monitoring systems are implemented either by writing kernel modules or by accessing proc files from user-space. Writing, distributing, and compiling kernel modules is not a task for everyone; it's a dangerous operation. They are not easy to maintain and debug either. However, the alternative might be even worse. To obtain the same kind of information, such as how many packets a card received in a second, you'd need to open and part a file, in this case */sys/class/net/eth0/statistics/rx_packets*. This might seem like a good idea, but it requires a lot of computing just to obtain some simple information, because using the open syscall is not cheap in some cases.

So, we need a solution that allows us to implement features similar to the ones of a kernel module without having to lose on performance. XDP is perfect for that, because we can use an XDP program to send the data we want to extract in a map. Then the map is consumed by a loader that can store the metrics into a storage backend and apply algorithms to it or plot the results in a graph.

DDoS Mitigation

Being able to see packets at the NIC level ensures that any possible packet is intercepted at the first stage, when the system didn't spend enough computing power yet to understand whether the packets will be useful for the system. In a typical scenario, a bpf map can instruct an XDP program to XDP_DROP packets from a certain source. That packet list can be generated in user-space after analyzing packets received via another map. Once there's a match between a packet flowing into the XDP program and an element of the list, the mitigation occurs. The packet is dropped, and the kernel didn't even need to spend a CPU cycle to handle it. That has the result of making the attacker goal difficult to achieve because, in this case, it wasn't able to waste any expensive computing resources.

Load Balancing

An interesting use case for XDP programs, is load balancing; however, XDP can retransmit packets only on the same NIC where they arrived. This means that XDP is not the best option to implement a classic load balancer that sits in front of all your servers and forwards traffic to them. However, this does not mean that XDP is not good for this use case. If we move load balancing from an external server to the same machines serving the application, you immediately see how their NICs can be used to do the job.

In that way, we can create a distributed load balancer where each machine hosting the application helps spread the traffic to the appropriate servers.

Firewalling

When people think of firewalling on Linux, they typically think of `iptables` or `net filter`. With XDP, you can get the same functionality in a completely programmable way directly in the NIC or its driver. Usually, firewalls are expensive machines sitting on top of the network stack or between nodes to control what their communication looks like. When using XDP, however, it's immediately clear that because XDP programs are very cheap and fast, we could implement the firewalling logic directly into a nodes' NICs instead of having a set of dedicated machines. A common use case is to have an XDP loader that controls a map with a set of rules changed with a remote procedure call API. The set of rules in the map then is dynamically passed to the XDP programs loaded into every specific machine, to control what it can receive, from who, and in which situation.

This alternative doesn't just make firewalling less expensive; it allows every node to deploy its own level of firewalling without relying on user-space software or the kernel to do that. When this is deployed using offloaded XDP as the operation mode, we obtain the maximum advantage because the processing is not even done by the main node CPU.

Conclusion

What great skills you have now! I promise that XDP will help you think about network flows in a completely different way from now on. Having to rely on tools like `iptables` or other user-space tools when dealing with network packets is often frustrating and slow. XDP is interesting because it is faster as a result of its direct packet processing capabilities, and because you can write your own logic to deal with the network packets. Because all of that arbitrary code can work with maps and interact with other BPF programs, you have an entire world of possible use cases to invent and explore for your own architectures!

Even though it is not about networking, the next chapter returns to a lot of the concepts covered here and in Chapter 6. Again, BPF is used to filter some conditions based on a given input and to filter what a program can do. Don't forget that the *F* in BPF stands for filter!

## CHAPTER 8

Linux Kernel Security, Capabilities, and Seccomp

BPF is a powerful way to extend the kernel without compromising stability, safety, and speed. For this reason, kernel developers thought that it would've been good to use its versatility to improve process isolation in Seccomp by implementing Seccomp filters backed by BPF programs, also known as Seccomp BPF. In this chapter we examine what Seccomp is and how it is used. Then you learn how to write Seccomp filters using BPF programs. After that you explore the built-in BPF hooks that the kernel has for Linux security modules.

Linux Security Modules (LSM) is a framework providing a set of functions that can be used to implement different security models in a standardized way. An LSM can be used in the kernel source tree directly, like Apparmor, SELinux, and Tomoyo.

We begin by discussing Linux capabilities.

Capabilities

The deal with Linux capabilities is that you need to provide your unprivileged process with permission to do a specific task, but you don't want to give suid privileges to the binary or otherwise make the process privileged, so you reduce the attack surface by just giving the process the specific capability to accomplish the specific tasks. For example, if your application needs to open a privileged port, like 80, instead of starting the process as root, you can just give it the CAP_NET_BIND_SERVICE capability.

Consider the following Go program called *main.go*:

```
package main

import (
```

```
        "net/http"
        "log"
)

func main() {
    log.Fatalf("%v", http.ListenAndServe(":80", nil))
}
```

This program serves an HTTPserver on port 80, a privileged port.

What we normally would do is to run that program straight after compiling it with the following:

```
$ go build -o capabilities main.go
$ ./capabilities
```

However, because we are not giving root privileges, that code will output an error when binding the port:

```
2019/04/25 23:17:06 listen tcp :80: bind: permission denied
exit status 1
```

 capsh (capability shell wrapper) is a tool that will start a shell with a specific set of capabilities.

In this case, as stated, instead of giving full root permissions, we can just allow the binding of privileged ports by allowing the cap_net_bind_service capability along with all the others the program already has. To do that, we can wrap our program run with capsh:

```
# capsh --caps='cap_net_bind_service+eip cap_setpcap,cap_setuid,cap_setgid+ep' \
    --keep=1 --user="nobody" \
    --addamb=cap_net_bind_service -- -c "./capabilities"
```

Let's break down that command a bit:

capsh
    We use capsh as wrapper.

--caps='cap_net_bind_service+eip cap_setpcap,cap_setuid,cap_setgid+ep'
    Because we need to change the user (we don't want to run as root), we need to specify cap_net_bind_service and the capabilities to actually do the user ID change from root to nobody, namely, cap_setuid and cap_setgid:

--keep=1
    We want to keep the set capabilities when the switch from root is done.

`--user="nobody"`
    The end user running our program will be nobody.

`--addamb=cap_net_bind_service`
    We set ambient capabilities because those are cleared after switching from root.

`-- -c "./capabilities"`
    After everything, we just run our program.

 Ambient capabilities are a specific kind of capability that is inherited by the children programs when the current program executes them using `execve()`. Only those capabilities that are permitted in the ambient and are inheritable can be ambient capabilities.

At this point, you are probably asking yourself what is that `+eip` after the capability in the `--caps` option. Those flags are used to determine whether:

- The capability needs to be activated (p).
- The capability is usable (e).
- The capability can be inherited by child processes (i).

Because we want to use our `cap_net_bind_service`, we need to make it e; then in our command, we started a shell. That then started the `capabilities` binary, and we needed to make it i. Finally, we want the capability to be activated (it was not because we changed the UID), using p. That ends up being `cap_net_bind_service+eip`.

You can verify that with `ss`; we're going to cut the output to make it fit in this page, but it will show the bound port and the user ID that are different than 0, in this case 65534:

```
# ss -tulpn -e -H | cut -d' ' -f17-
128    *:80    *:*
users:(("capabilities",pid=30040,fd=3)) uid:65534 ino:11311579 sk:2c v6only:0
```

We used `capsh` for this example, but you can write the wrapper by using *libcap*; for more info, see `man 3 libcap`.

When writing programs, it's fairly common that the developer doesn't really know in advance all the capabilities needed by a program at runtime; moreover, with newer releases, those capabilities might change.

To better understand the capabilities used by our program, we can use the `capable` tool from BCC that sets up a kprobe on the kernel function `cap_capable`:

```
/usr/share/bcc/tools/capable
TIME      UID   PID    TID    COMM             CAP   NAME                  AUDIT
10:12:53  0     424    424    systemd-udevd    12    CAP_NET_ADMIN         1
10:12:57  0     1103   1101   timesync         25    CAP_SYS_TIME          1
10:12:57  0     19545  19545  capabilities     10    CAP_NET_BIND_SERVICE  1
```

We can accomplish the same using `bpftrace` with a one-liner kprobe on the `cap_capable` kernel function:

```
bpftrace -e \
    'kprobe:cap_capable {
        time("%H:%M:%S  ");
        printf("%-6d %-6d %-16s %-4d %d\n", uid, pid, comm, arg2, arg3);
    }' \
    | grep -i capabilities
```

That will output something like the following, if our program `capabilities` is started after the kprobe:

```
12:01:56  1000   13524  capabilities     21  0
12:01:56  1000   13524  capabilities     21  0
12:01:56  1000   13524  capabilities     21  0
12:01:56  1000   13524  capabilities     12  0
12:01:56  1000   13524  capabilities     12  0
12:01:56  1000   13524  capabilities     12  0
12:01:56  1000   13524  capabilities     12  0
12:01:56  1000   13524  capabilities     10  1
```

The fifth column is the capability required by the process, and because this output also includes nonaudit events, we see all the nonaudit checks and finally the required capability with the audit flag (the last in the previous output) set to 1. The capability we are interested in is CAP_NET_BIND_SERVICE, which is defined as a constant in the kernel source code at `include/uapi/linux/capability.h` and has ID 10:

```
/* Allows binding to TCP/UDP sockets below 1024 */
/* Allows binding to ATM VCIs below 32 */

#define CAP_NET_BIND_SERVICE 10
```

Capabilities are often used in container runtimes, like runC or Docker, to make containers unprivileged and allow only the capabilities needed to run the majority of applications. When an application needs particular capabilities, in Docker that can be done with `--cap-add`:

```
docker run -it --rm --cap-add=NET_ADMIN ubuntu ip link add dummy0 type dummy
```

This command will give the CAP_NET_ADMIN capability to that container, allowing it to set up a netlink to add the dummy0 interface.

The next section shows how to achieve capabilities such as filtering but by using another technique that will let us programmatically implement our own filters.

Seccomp

Seccomp stands for Secure Computing, and it is a security layer implemented in the Linux kernel that allows developers to filter specific syscalls. Although Seccomp is comparable to capabilities, its ability to control specific system calls makes it a lot more flexible when compared to capabilities.

Seccomp and capabilites do not exclude each other; they are often used together to bring benefits from both the worlds. For example, you might want to give the CAP_NET_ADMIN capability to a process but not allow it to accept connections on a socket by blocking the accept and accept4 syscalls.

The way Seccomp filters is based on BPF filters using the SECCOMP_MODE_FILTER mode, and syscalls filtering is done in the same way it is for packets.

Seccomp filters are loaded using prctl via the PR_SET_SECCOMP operation; those filters are expressed in the form of a BPF program that is executed on each Seccomp *packet* expressed using the seccomp_data struct. That struct contains the reference architecture, the CPU instruction pointer at the time of the syscall, and a maximum of six system call arguments expressed as uint64.

Here's how the seccomp_data struct looks from the kernel's source at linux/seccomp.h:

```
struct seccomp_data {
        int nr;
        __u32 arch;
        __u64 instruction_pointer;
        __u64 args[6];
};
```

As you can see by reading the struct, we can filter based on the syscall, based on its arguments, or based on a combination of them.

After receiving each Seccomp packet, the filter has the duty of doing the processing to make a final decision to tell the kernel what to do next. The final decision is expressed via one of the return values (status codes) it can give, as described here:

SECCOMP_RET_KILL_PROCESS
> It will kill the whole process immediately after filtering the syscall, which as a consequence, is not executed.

SECCOMP_RET_KILL_THREAD
> It will kill the current thread immediately after filtering the syscall, which as a consequence, is not executed.

SECCOMP_RET_KILL
> This is an alias to SECCOMP_RET_KILL_THREAD left for compatibility.

SECCOMP_RET_TRAP

The syscall is disallowed, and the SIGSYS (Bad System Call) signal is sent to the task calling it.

SECCOMP_RET_ERRNO

The syscall is not executed, and the SECCOMP_RET_DATA part of the filter's return value is passed to user-space as the errno value. Depending on what was the cause of the error, a different errno is returned. You can find the list of error numbers in the following section.

SECCOMP_RET_TRACE

This is used to notify a ptrace tracer using PTRACE_O_TRACESECCOMP to intercept when the syscall is called to observe and control the execution of the syscall. In case there's no tracer attached, an error is returned, errno is set to -ENOSYS, and the syscall is not executed.

SECCOMP_RET_LOG

The syscall is allowed and logged.

SECCOMP_RET_ALLOW

The syscall is just allowed.

 ptrace is a system call used to implement tracing mechanisms on a process, called the *tracee*, with the effect of being able to observe and control the process's execution. The tracer program can effectively affect the execution and change the memory registers of the tracee. In the context of Seccomp, ptrace is used when triggered by the SECCOMP_RET_TRACE status code; therefore, the tracer can prevent the syscall from executing and implement its own logic.

Seccomp Errors

From time to time, while working with Seccomp you will encounter different errors given by the return value of type SECCOMP_RET_ERRNO. To notify that an error happened, the seccomp syscall will return -1 instead of 0.

The possible errors are as follows:

EACCESS

The caller is not allowed to do the syscall—usually this happens because it didn't have CAP_SYS_ADMIN privileges or did not set no_new_privs with prctl, which we explain later in this chapter.

EFAULT

The passed arguments (args in the seccomp_data struct) did not have a valid address.

EINVAL

It can have four meanings:

- The requested operation is not known or supported by this kernel within its current configuration.
- The specified flags are not valid for the requested operation.
- Operation includes BPF_ABS, but there are problems with the specified offset that might exceed the size of the seccomp_data structure.
- The number of instructions passed to the filter exceeds the maximum number of instructions.

ENOMEM

There's not enough memory to execute the program.

EOPNOTSUPP

The operation specified that with SECCOMP_GET_ACTION_AVAIL, the action was available, but in reality the kernel has no support for the return action in the arguments.

ESRCH

There was a problem during the synchronization of another thread.

ENOSYS

There's no tracer attached to the SECCOMP_RET_TRACE action.

 prctl is a syscall that allows a user-space program to control (set and get) specific aspects of a process, such as endian-ness, thread names, secure computing (Seccomp) mode, privileges, Perf events, and so on.

Seccomp might sound to you like it is a sandboxing mechanism, but that's not true. Seccomp is a utility that lets its users develop a sandboxing mechanism. Now here's how to write programs to write the custom interactions using a filter called directly by a Seccomp syscall.

Seccomp BPF Filter Example

In this example we show how to put together the two actions described earlier:

- Write the Seccomp BPF program to be used as a filter with different return codes based on the decisions it makes.
- Load the filter using prctl.

First the example needs some headers from the standard library and the Linux kernel:

```
#include <errno.h>
#include <linux/audit.h>
#include <linux/bpf.h>
#include <linux/filter.h>
#include <linux/seccomp.h>
#include <linux/unistd.h>
#include <stddef.h>
#include <stdio.h>
#include <stdlib.h>
#include <sys/prctl.h>
#include <unistd.h>
```

Before trying to execute this example, we need to make sure that our kernel has been compiled with CONFIG_SECCOMP and CONFIG_SECCOMP_FILTER set to y. In a live machine, that can be checked with the following:

```
cat /proc/config.gz| zcat  | grep -i CONFIG_SECCOMP
```

The rest of the code is the install_filter function, made up of two parts. The first part contains our the list of BPF filtering instructions:

```
static int install_filter(int nr, int arch, int error) {
  struct sock_filter filter[] = {
    BPF_STMT(BPF_LD + BPF_W + BPF_ABS, (offsetof(struct seccomp_data, arch))),
    BPF_JUMP(BPF_JMP + BPF_JEQ + BPF_K, arch, 0, 3),
    BPF_STMT(BPF_LD + BPF_W + BPF_ABS, (offsetof(struct seccomp_data, nr))),
    BPF_JUMP(BPF_JMP + BPF_JEQ + BPF_K, nr, 0, 1),
    BPF_STMT(BPF_RET + BPF_K, SECCOMP_RET_ERRNO | (error & SECCOMP_RET_DATA)),
    BPF_STMT(BPF_RET + BPF_K, SECCOMP_RET_ALLOW),
  };
```

The instructions are set up using the BPF_STMT and BPF_JUMP macros defined in linux/filter.h.

Let's walk through the instructions:

BPF_STMT(BPF_LD + BPF_W + BPF_ABS (offsetof(struct seccomp_data, arch)))
   This loads and accumulates with BPF_LD in the form of the word BPF_W, and the packet data is contained at the fixed BPF_ABS offset.

```
BPF_JUMP(BPF_JMP + BPF_JEQ + BPF_K, arch, 0, 3)
```
This checks with BPF_JEQ whether the architecture value in the accumulator constant BPF_K is equal to arch. If so, it will jump with offset zero to the next instruction; otherwise, it will jump with offset three to give an error, in this case because the arch did not match.

```
BPF_STMT(BPF_LD + BPF_W + BPF_ABS (offsetof(struct seccomp_data, nr)))
```
This loads and accumulates with BPF_LD in the form of the word BPF_W, which is the syscall number data contained at the fixed BPF_ABS offset.

```
BPF_JUMP(BPF_JMP + BPF_JEQ + BPF_K, nr, 0, 1)
```
This compares the value from the syscall number to the one in the nr variable. If they are equal, it will go to the next instruction and disallow the syscall; otherwise, it will allow the syscall with SECCOMP_RET_ALLOW.

```
BPF_STMT(BPF_RET + BPF_K, SECCOMP_RET_ERRNO | (error &
SECCOMP_RET_DATA))
```
This terminates the program with BPF_RET and gives as a result an error, SEC COMP_RET_ERRNO, with the specified error number from the err variable.

```
BPF_STMT(BPF_RET + BPF_K, SECCOMP_RET_ALLOW)
```
This terminates the program with BPF_RET and allows the syscall execution using SECCOMP_RET_ALLOW.

Seccomp Is cBPF

At this point you might wondering why a list of instructions is used instead of a compiled ELF object or a C program that is then JIT compiled to it?

There are two reasons:

- The first is that Seccomp uses cBPF (classic BPF) and not eBPF, which means that it does not have registries but just an accumulator to store the last computation result, as you can notice in the example.

- The second is that Seccomp accepts a pointer to an array of BPF instructions directly and nothing else. The macros we used are just helpers to specify those instructions in a programmer-friendly way.

If you need further assistance in understanding that assembly, you will probably find useful some pseudocode that does the same thing:

```
if (arch != AUDIT_ARCH_X86_64) {
    return SECCOMP_RET_ALLOW;
}
```

```
    if (nr == __NR_write) {
        return SECCOMP_RET_ERRNO;
    }
    return SECCOMP_RET_ALLOW;
```

After defining the filter code in the socket_filter struct, we need to define a sock_fprog containing the filter code and the calculated length of the filter itself. This data structure is needed as an argument for declaring the process operation later:

```
struct sock_fprog prog = {
  .len = (unsigned short)(sizeof(filter) / sizeof(filter[0])),
  .filter = filter,
};
```

Now we have only one thing left to do in the install_filter function: load the program itself! To do that, we use prctl using PR_SET_SECCOMP as an option because we want to enter secure computing mode. Then we instruct the mode to load a filter with SECCOMP_MODE_FILTER that is contained in our prog variable of type sock_fprog:

```
if (prctl(PR_SET_SECCOMP, SECCOMP_MODE_FILTER, &prog)) {
  perror("prctl(PR_SET_SECCOMP)");
  return 1;
}
return 0;
}
```

Finally, we can take advantage of our install_filter function, but before using it, we need to use prctl to set PR_SET_NO_NEW_PRIVS on the current execution to avoid the situation in which child processes can have wider privileges than the parent. This lets us make the following prctl calls in the install_filter function without root privileges.

We can now call the install_filter function. We will block all the write syscalls relative to the X86-64 architecture and will just give permission denied to all the attempts. After the filter installation we just continue the execution by using the first argument:

```
int main(int argc, char const *argv[]) {
  if (prctl(PR_SET_NO_NEW_PRIVS, 1, 0, 0, 0)) {
    perror("prctl(NO_NEW_PRIVS)");
    return 1;
  }
  install_filter(__NR_write, AUDIT_ARCH_X86_64, EPERM);
  return system(argv[1]);
}
```

Let's try it now!

To compile our program, we can use either clang or gcc; either way, it's just a matter of compiling the main.c file with no special options:

```
clang main.c -o filter-write
```

We said that we blocked all the writes in our program. To test it then, we need a program that does writes; the ls program seems like a good candidate, and here is how it behaves normally:

```
ls -la
total 36
drwxr-xr-x 2 fntlnz users  4096 Apr 28 21:09 .
drwxr-xr-x 4 fntlnz users  4096 Apr 26 13:01 ..
-rwxr-xr-x 1 fntlnz users 16800 Apr 28 21:09 filter-write
-rw-r--r-- 1 fntlnz users    19 Apr 28 21:09 .gitignore
-rw-r--r-- 1 fntlnz users  1282 Apr 28 21:08 main.c
```

Cool! Here's what our wrapper program usage looks like; we just pass the program we want to test as first argument:

```
./filter-write "ls -la"
```

After it's executed, that program gives completely empty output, leaving no output. However, we can use strace to see what's happening:

```
strace -f ./filter-write "ls -la"
```

The result had been stripped of a lot of noise, and the relevant part of that shows that writes are being blocked with an EPERM error, which is the same one we set up. This means the program is silent because it can't access that syscall now:

```
[pid 25099] write(2, "ls: ", 4)          = -1 EPERM (Operation not permitted)
[pid 25099] write(2, "write error", 11) = -1 EPERM (Operation not permitted)
[pid 25099] write(2, "\n", 1)            = -1 EPERM (Operation not permitted)
```

You now have an understanding of how Seccomp BPF operates and a good sense of what you can do with it. But wouldn't it be good if there were a way to achieve the same using eBPF instead of cBPF to harness its power?

When thinking about eBPF programs, most people think that you just write them and load them with root privileges. Although that statement is generally true, the kernel implements a set of mechanisms to protect eBPF objects at various levels; those mechanisms are called BPF LSM *hooks*.

BPF LSM Hooks

To provide architecture-independent control over system events, LSM implements the concept of hooks. Technically, a hook call is similar to a syscall; however, being system independent and integrated with the LSM framework makes hooks interesting because the layer of abstraction this provides can be convenient and can help avoid the kind of troubles that can occur when working with syscalls on different architectures.

At the time of writing, the kernel has seven hooks related to BPF programs, and SELinux is the only in-tree LSM implementing them.

You can see this in the kernel source tree in this file: `include/linux/security.h`:

```
extern int security_bpf(int cmd, union bpf_attr *attr, unsigned int size);
extern int security_bpf_map(struct bpf_map *map, fmode_t fmode);
extern int security_bpf_prog(struct bpf_prog *prog);
extern int security_bpf_map_alloc(struct bpf_map *map);
extern void security_bpf_map_free(struct bpf_map *map);
extern int security_bpf_prog_alloc(struct bpf_prog_aux *aux);
extern void security_bpf_prog_free(struct bpf_prog_aux *aux);
```

Each one of those hooks will be invoked at different stages of the execution:

security_bpf
> Does an initial check on the executed BPF syscalls

security_bpf_map
> Does a check when the kernel returns a file descriptor for a map

security_bpf_prog
> Does a check when the kernel returns a file descriptor for an eBPF program

security_bpf_map_alloc
> Does the initialization of the security field inside BPF maps

security_bpf_map_free
> Does the cleanup of the security field inside BPF maps

security_bpf_prog_alloc
> Does the initialization of the security field inside BPF programs

security_bpf_prog_free
> Does the cleanup of the security field inside BPF programs

Now that we've seen them, it becomes clear that the idea behind the LSM BPF hooks is that they can provide a per-object protection for eBPF objects in order to ensure that only those with the appropriate privileges can do operations on maps and programs.

Conclusion

Security is not something that you can implement in a universal way for everything you want to protect. It is important to be able to secure systems at different layers and in different ways, and, believe it or not, the best way to secure a system is to stack different layers with different perspectives so that a compromised layer does not lead to the ability to access the entire system. The kernel developers did a great job in providing us with a set of different layers and interaction points that we can use; our hope is that we gave you a good understanding of what the layers are and how to use BPF programs to interact with them.

## CHAPTER 9

Real-World Use Cases

The most important question to ask yourself when implementing a new technology is: "What are the use cases for this out there?" That's why we decided to interview the creators of some of the most exciting BPF projects out there to share their ideas.

Sysdig eBPF God Mode

Sysdig, the company that makes the eponymous open source Linux troubleshooting tool, started playing with eBPF in 2017 under kernel 4.11.

It has been historically using a kernel module to extract and do all the kernel-side work, but as the user base increased and when more and more companies started experimenting, the company acknowledged that it is a limitation for the majority of external actors, in many ways:

- There's an increasing number of users who can't load kernel modules on their machines. Cloud-native platforms are becoming more and more restrictive against what runtime programs can do.

- New contributors (and even old) don't understand the architecture of a kernel module. That decreases the overall number of contributors and is a limiting factor for the growth of the project itself.

- Kernel modules maintenance is difficult, not just because of writing the code, but also because of the effort needed to keep it safe and well organized.

For those motivations, Sysdig decided to try the approach of writing the same set of features it has in the module but using an eBPF program instead. Another benefit that automatically comes from adopting eBPF is the possibility for Sysdig to further take advantage of other nice eBPF tracing features. For example, it's relatively easy to attach eBPF programs to particular execution points in a user-space application using user probes, as described in "User-Space Probes" on page 53.

In addition, the project can now use native helper capabilities in eBPF programs to capture stack traces of running processes to augment the typical system call event stream. This gives users even more troubleshooting information.

Although it's all bells and whistles now, Sysdig initially faced some challenges due to the limitations of the eBPF virtual machine when getting started, so the chief architect of the project, Gianluca Borello, decided to improve it by contributing upstream patches to the kernel itself, including:

- The ability to deal with strings in eBPF programs natively (*https://oreil.ly/ZJ09y*)

- Multiple patches to improve the arguments semantic in eBPF programs 1 (*https://oreil.ly/lPcGT*), 2 (*https://oreil.ly/5S_tR*), and 3 (*https://oreil.ly/HLrEu*)

The latter was particularly essential to dealing with system call arguments, probably the most important data source available in the tool.

Figure 9-1 shows the architecture of the eBPF mode in Sysdig.

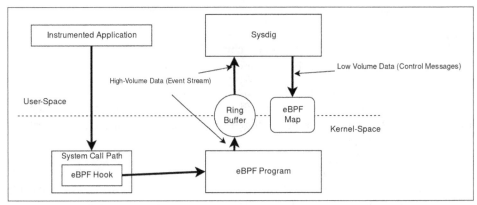

Figure 9-1. Sysdig's eBPF architecture

The core of the implementation is a collection of custom eBPF programs responsible for the instrumentation. These programs are written in a subset of the C programming language. They are compiled using recent versions of Clang and LLVM, which translate the high-level C code into the eBPF bytecode.

There is one eBPF program for every different execution point where Sysdig instruments the kernel. Currently, eBPF programs are attached to the following static tracepoints:

- System call entry path

- System call exit path
- Process context switch
- Process termination
- Minor and major page faults
- Process signal delivery

Each program takes in the execution point data (e.g., for system calls, arguments passed by the calling process) and starts processing them. The processing depends on the type of system call. For simple system calls, the arguments are just copied verbatim into an eBPF map used for temporary storage until the entire event frame is formed. For other, more complicated calls, the eBPF programs include the logic to translate or augment the arguments. This enables the Sysdig application in user-space to fully leverage the data.

Some of the additional data includes the following:

- Data associated to a network connection (TCP/UDP IPv4/IPv6 tuple, UNIX socket names, etc.)
- Highly granular metrics about the process (memory counters, page faults, socket queue length, etc.)
- Container-specific data, such as the cgroups the process issuing the syscall belongs to, as well as the namespaces in which process lives

As shown in Figure 9-1, after an eBPF program captures all the needed data for a specific system call, it uses a special native BPF function to push the data to a set of per-CPU ring buffers that the user-space application can read at a very high throughput. This is where the usage of eBPF in Sysdig differs from the typical paradigm of using eBPF maps to share "small data" produced in kernel-space with user-space. To learn more about maps and how to communicate between user- and kernel-space, refer to Chapter 3.

From a performance point of view, the results are good! In Figure 9-2 you can see how the instrumentation overhead of the eBPF instrumentation of Sysdig is only marginally greater than the "classic" kernel module instrumentation.

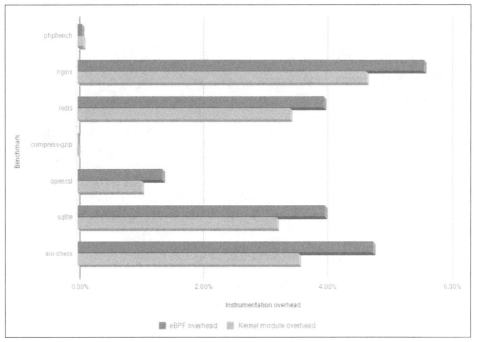

Figure 9-2. Sysdig eBPF performance comparison

You can play with Sysdig and its eBPF support by following the usage instructions (*https://oreil.ly/luHKp*), but also make sure to also look at the code of the BPF driver (*https://oreil.ly/AJddM*).

Flowmill

Flowmill, an observability startup, emerged from an academic research project called Flowtune (*https://oreil.ly/e9heR*) by its founder, Jonathan Perry. Flowtune examined how to efficiently schedule individual packets in congested datacenter networks. One of the core pieces of technology required for this work was a means of gathering network telemetry with extremely low overhead. Flowmill ultimately adapted this technology to observe, aggregate, and analyze connections between every component in a distributed application to do the following:

- Provide an accurate view of how services interact in a distributed system
- Identify areas where statistically significant changes have occurred in traffic rates, errors, or latency

Flowmill uses eBPF kernel probes to trace every open socket and capture operating systems metrics on them periodically. This is complex for a number of reasons:

- It's necessary to instrument both new connections and existing connections already open at the time the eBPF probes are established. Additionally, it must account for both TCP and UDP as well as IPv4 and IPv6 code paths through the kernel.

- For container-based systems, each socket must be attributed to the appropriate cgroup and joined with orchestrator metadata from a platform like Kubernetes or Docker.

- Network address translation performed via conntrack must be instrumented to establish the mapping between sockets and their externally visible IP addresses. For example, in Docker, a common networking model uses source NAT to masquerade containers behind a host IP address and in Kubernetes, and a service virtual IP address is used to represent a set of containers.

- Data collected by eBPF programs must be post-processed to provide aggregates by service and to match data collected on two sides of a connection.

However, adding eBPF kernel probes provides a far more efficient and robust way of gathering this data. It completely eliminates the risk of missing connections and can be done with low overhead on every socket on a subsecond interval. Flowmill's approach relies on an agent, which combines a set of eBPF kprobes and user-space metrics collection as well as off-box aggregation and post processing. The implementation makes heavy use of Perf rings to pass metrics collected on each socket to user-space for further processing. Additionally, it uses a hash map to keep track of open TCP and UDP sockets.

Flowmill found there are generally two strategies to designing eBPF instrumentation. The "easy" approach finds the one to two kernel functions that are called on every instrumented event, but requires BPF code to maintain more state and to do more work per call, on an instrumentation point called very frequently. To alleviate concerns about instrumentation impacting production workloads, Flowmill followed the other strategy: instrument more specific functions that are called less frequently and signify an important event. This has significantly lower overhead, but requires more effort in covering all important code paths, especially across kernel versions as kernel code evolves.

For example, `tcp_v4_do_rcv` captures all established TCP RX traffic and has access to the `struct sock`, but has extremely high call volume. Instead, users can instrument functions dealing with ACKs, out-of-order packet handling, RTT estimation, and more that allow handling specific events that influence known metrics.

With this approach across TCP, UDP, processes, containers, conntrack, and other subsystems, the system achieves extremely good performance of the system with overhead low enough that is difficult to measure in most systems. CPU overhead is generally 0.1% to 0.25% per core including eBPF and user-space components and is dependent primarily on the rate at which new sockets are created.

There is more about Flowmill and Flowtune on their website (*https://www.flow mill.com*).

Sysdig and Flowmill are pioneers in the use of BPF to build monitoring and observability tools, but they are not the only ones. Throughout the book, we've mentioned other companies like Cillium and Facebook that have adopted BPF as their framework of choice to deliver highly secure and performant networking infrastructure. We're very excited for the future ahead of BPF and its community, and we cannot wait to see what you built with it.

Index

different behaviors with different types of
maps, 32
BPF_F_USER_STACK flag, 64
bpf_get_current_comm function, 50
bpf_get_current_pid_tgid function, 54
BPF_HASH macro, 68
BPF_HISTOGRAM macro, 68
bpf_lpm_trie_key struct, 38
bpf_map_create helper function, 23
bpf_map_def struct, 100
bpf_map_delete_element function, 27
bpf_map_get_next_key function, 29
bpf_map_lookup_and_delete function, 41
    using with stack maps, 42
bpf_map_lookup_and_delete_element func-
    tion, 30
bpf_map_lookup_elem helper function, 26, 34,
    100
bpf_map_lookup_elem_flags function, 32
BPF_MAP_TYPE_ARRAY, 99
BPF_MAP_TYPE_ARRAY_OF_MAPS type, 39
BPF_MAP_TYPE_CGROUP_STORAGE type,
    40
BPF_MAP_TYPE_CPUMAP type, 39
BPF_MAP_TYPE_DEVMAP type, 39
BPF_MAP_TYPE_HASH type, 33
BPF_MAP_TYPE_HASH_OF_MAPS type, 39
BPF_MAP_TYPE_LPM_TRIE type, 38
BPF_MAP_TYPE_LRU_HASH type, 38
BPF_MAP_TYPE_LRU_PERCPU_HASH type,
    38
BPF_MAP_TYPE_PERCPU_ARRAY type, 37,
    124
BPF_MAP_TYPE_PERCPU_CGROUP_
    STORAGE type, 40
BPF_MAP_TYPE_PERCPU_HASH type, 37
BPF_MAP_TYPE_PERF_EVENT_ARRAY
    type, 36
BPF_MAP_TYPE_PROG_ARRAY type, 34
BPF_MAP_TYPE_QUEUE type, 41
BPF_MAP_TYPE_REUSEPORT_SOCKAR-
    RAY type, 41
BPF_MAP_TYPE_SOCKHASH type, 40
BPF_MAP_TYPE_SOCKMAP type, 40
BPF_MAP_TYPE_STACK type, 42
BPF_MAP_TYPE_STACK_TRACE type, 37, 63
BPF_MAP_TYPE_XSKMAP type, 40
bpf_map_update_elem function, 24, 100
    BPF_F_LOCK flag, 32

using with queue maps, 41
using with stack maps, 42
BPF_OBJ_GET command, 44
BPF_PERF_OUTPUT macro, 70
BPF_PIN_FD command, 44
BPF_PROG_TEST_RUN command, 127
BPF_PROG_TYPE_SOCKET_FILTER type,
    92, 97-102
BPF_PROG_TYPE_XDP, 126
bpf_redirect_map function, 39
bpf_spin_lock function, 31
bpf_spin_unlock function, 31
BPF_STACK_TRACE macro, 63
BPF_STMT and BPF_JUMP macros, 142
BPF_TABLE macro, 124
bpf_tail_call function, 35
bpf_trace_printk function, 51
BTF (BPF Type Format), 19
    annotating a map with, 31
    displaying information about with BPFTool,
        82
btf subcommand (bpftool), 82
busy polling mode (XDP), 117

C

C language
    annotating C types with BPF Type Format,
        19
    BPF programs for Traffic Control, 107
    BPF programs in, 8
    Python conversion to C types with ctypes
        library, 129
capabilities, 135-138
    ambient, 137
    capable tool in BCC, 137
    CAP_NET_BIND_SERVICE, 135
    Seccomp and, 139
    use in container runtimes, 138
capsh (capability shell wrapper), 136
cap_capable function, 137
CAP_NET_ADMIN capability, 138
cBPF (classic BPF), 92, 143
cgroup array maps, 37
cgroup device programs, 14
cgroup open socket programs, 13
cgroup socket address programs, 15
cgroup socket programs, 13
cgroup storage maps, 40
cgroups, 2

About the Authors

David Calavera works as CTO at Netlify. He's served as the maintainer of Docker and contributor to Runc, Go, and BCC tools as well as other open source projects. He's known for his work on the Docker projects, building and fostering the Docker plug-in ecosystem. David has a strong fondness for flame graphs and performance optimizations.

Lorenzo Fontana is on the Open Source Team at Sysdig where he primarily works on Falco, a Cloud Native Computing Foundation project that does container runtime security and anomaly detection through a kernel module and eBPF. He's passionate about distributed systems, software-defined networking, the Linux kernel, and performance analysis.

Colophon

The bird on the cover of *Linux Observability with BPF* is a Sunda scops owl (*Otus lempiji*). Scops are small owls with *aigrettes*, or tufts of feathers on the head. Sunda scops owls are native to southeast Asia and are also known as Singapore scops owls. Historically, Sunda scops owls live in forests, but they have adapted with urbanization and also live in gardens today.

Sunda scops owls are light brown with black speckles and streaks. They reach about eight inches in height and six ounces in weight. In early spring, the female owls lay two to three eggs in tree hollows. They eat insects (especially beetles) but also hunt rodents, lizards, and small birds.

The piercing cry of a Sunda scops owl is so distinctive that they are commonly called screech owls. Their screech reaches a high pitch at its end and can be repeated as often as every 10 seconds.

Many of the animals on O'Reilly covers are endangered; all of them are important to the world.

The cover illustration is by Suzy Wiviott, based on a black and white engraving from *British Birds*. The cover fonts are Gilroy Semibold and Guardian Sans. The text font is Adobe Minion Pro; the heading font is Adobe Myriad Condensed; and the code font is Dalton Maag's Ubuntu Mono.

O'REILLY®

There's much more where this came from.

Experience books, videos, live online training courses, and more from O'Reilly and our 200+ partners—all in one place.

Learn more at oreilly.com/online-learning